Theatre: A Very Short Introduction

VERY SHORT INTRODUCTIONS are for anyone wanting a stimulating and accessible way in to a new subject. They are written by experts, and have been translated into more than 40 different languages.

The Series began in 1995, and now covers a wide variety of topics in every discipline. The VSI library now contains over 350 volumes—a Very Short Introduction to everything from Psychology and Philosophy of Science to American History and Relativity—and continues to grow in every subject area.

Very Short Introductions available now:

Available soon:

For more information visit our website

www.oup.com/vsi/

Marvin Carlson

THEATRE

A Very Short Introduction

OXFORD
UNIVERSITY PRESS

OXFORD
UNIVERSITY PRESS

Great Clarendon Street, Oxford, OX2 6DP,
United Kingdom

Oxford University Press is a department of the University of Oxford.
It furthers the University's objective of excellence in research, scholarship,
and education by publishing worldwide. Oxford is a registered trade mark of
Oxford University Press in the UK and in certain other countries

Published in the United States of America by Oxford University Press
198 Madison Avenue, New York, NY 10016, United States of America

British Library Cataloguing in Publication Data
Data available

Library of Congress Control Number: 2014939000

ISBN 978–0–19–966982–0

Printed in Great Britain by
Ashford Colour Press Ltd, Gosport, Hampshire.

Contents

List of illustrations

Chapter 1
What is theatre?

The origins of what is today called theatre go far back before recorded history. Theatre is built upon what appear to be universal human activities and there has been endless and ultimately fruitless discussion concerning which of these activities was the true basis of theatre. Likely the best answer is that these activities combined and developed in countless different ways in different communities and cultures, resulting in the modern world in a vast array of theatre and theatre-related forms.

Imitation

One of these basic activities is clearly imitation. Paleolithic cave paintings provide indisputable evidence of the antiquity of this interest, and whatever we know or can speculate about early humans indicates that this fascination with imitation was not confined to graphic representation, but was also carried out as an embodied practice. Supernatural figures, animals, and iconic human figures surely were represented by performers within their community just as they are represented on the walls of Paleolithic caves. Another activity found in all human cultures is some form of storytelling. Among the most ancient forms of the story that we know are the cultural myths, stories of the gods, of how the world and man came to be and of the dynamics of human interaction and of man's interaction with the world. Usually the person telling these stories holds a special position in the society, sometimes simply an entertainer but also at times a seer, a guide, a shaman. There has always been a close connection between imitation and storytelling. An important part of storytelling has been the assumption of various roles and voices by the storyteller, and one may consider much theatre as built of the same material as storytelling, but enacted imitatively with entire bodies rather than in the inflections of a single voice.

One of the best-known basic formulas of drama was provided by theorist Eric Bentley in 1965: 'A impersonates B while C looks on.' The two verbs are key, with the first stressing the idea of active imitation and the second that of spectatorship. Simple as this formula is, it allows an important distinction to be made between such closely related forms as dance and storytelling (with the important proviso that both can move within the realm of theatre if 'impersonation' is involved). The formula assumes, of course, that A, B, and C are all humans, and this is essentially true, though there have been plays in which human actors impersonated animals, insects, birds, plants, and even inanimate objects.

In fact, A need not be human either, and in a significant part of the world is not. A may be an inanimate object manipulated by a human, in short a puppet. Puppet theatre in the Western world has often been considered a minor form, suitable for children or simple folk entertainment, but not worthy of consideration by serious students of theatre. This attitude seems to be in the process of changing, however, with puppet theatre growing in respectability, visibility, and sophistication, and as Western audiences become more aware of the rich puppet theatre traditions in other parts of the world. It should also be noted that while Bentley's definition covers the essential matters of imitation and spectatorship, it excludes the crucial other component, storytelling. Hence we should add the insight of Aristotle, to create a formula more like 'A imitates B *performing an action* while C looks on.'

The boundaries of theatre

Although performance of some kind seems to be universal in world cultures, the particular combination of elements that has come to be known as theatre is much more limited, though it has developed in various ways in many parts of the world. Both the word and the concept of theatre are rooted in Western culture and practice, and although this study will attempt a global consideration of this art, it must recognize at the beginning certain sometimes rather arbitrary boundaries that the Western tradition has imposed upon it. For example, within the Western tradition, theatre and opera are traditionally studied as essentially separate forms, students of the first focusing upon the words, and of the second upon the music, despite the many obvious overlaps. Dance, though not only closely related to theatre and often embedded within it, is also largely omitted from theatre studies. Given the limited size of this study I will reluctantly to a large extent follow this tradition, while recognizing that in most parts of the world such distinctions have not been followed except under the influence of colonialism. I will address these and related problems, however, in my section on theatre and performance.

My discussion of how the form we call theatre has been developed in various world cultures will be pursued in a roughly chronological form. Many theatre histories begin with ancient Egypt ritual, which I will address in my next chapter but not here, since the earliest culture to fully develop the form we now call theatre, and the one most instrumental in spreading the concept of this form first through Europe and subsequently to other parts of the world, was classical Greece, during the 5th century BCE. Many different theories have been advanced about the origin of Greek theatre, but all have been challenged and there is simply not enough known about the cultural life of that period to settle the question definitively. In any case, by the mid 5th century theatre was well established as a cultural form, with highly codified rules for the creation of its texts, the costuming of its

3

actors, and its means of presentation. The form was developed in the city of Athens, and spread outward to its colonies. Theatre was a major part of a number of Greek festivals, and three types of drama, the tragedy, comedy, and satyr play, were presented in these festivals in competition for honour and prizes. Though little is known of the performance style, there are many artistic representations of the actors, informing us that they wore elaborate costumes and masks. An important feature of the presentations was a chorus, which sang and danced.

Classical Greece and Rome

Both Greek and Roman theatres were open-air municipal structures for very large audiences. Every Greek city of any size possessed a monumental space, often dug into a hillside, for theatre, and the ruins of these can still be found throughout Greece and its colonies. The excavated area was a semicircle of stone benches, providing seating for the audience. This sloped down to a flat circular area, the orchestra, where the chorus performed. Beyond the orchestra was the structure built for the actors, the skene, from which comes the modern word scene. The area in front of the skene house, at first level with the orchestra, but later raised to a higher level more suggestive of a modern stage, was the proskenion, from which comes the modern word proscenium, for the arch surrounding the modern stage (Figure 1).

Although the great age of Greek playwriting was confined to the 5th century BCE, the theatre continued to be an important part of Greek life, and indeed with the conquest of Alexander the Great in the next century, this tradition was carried further around the Mediterranean and as far east as Syria and Iraq. The theatres of the Hellenistic period did not radically change in form, although by that time a raised proscenium was universal and some stages had become more elaborate, containing two or even three storeys. Plays of the classical period continued to be performed, although the fanciful comedies of Aristophanes lost their popularity to a

1. Greek theatre at Epidauros

new style of comedy, diminishing the role of the chorus, and moving away from satires of particular living targets to depictions of more general or stock characters. Hellenistic scholars divided comedy into old, middle, and new styles, the old represented by Aristophanes and his contemporaries, the middle by the changes just noted, and the new by a group of dramatists of the late 4th and 3rd centuries BCE, the best known of whom was Menander.

No examples of middle comedy survive, but one complete play by Menander, *Dyskolos*, was discovered in the mid 20th century. New comedy was primarily characterized by its focus on contemporary bourgeois life. Its basic plot structures and stock characters were picked up and utilized by the major Roman comic dramatists, Plautus and Terence, and through them were disseminated by Renaissance dramatists throughout Europe. As a result, these stock characters and plot arrangements have remained an important element of the European comic tradition

5

into modern times. The most common plots concerned a pair of thwarted young lovers, struggling against recalcitrant members of the older generation and grotesque would-be rivals and aided by an array of servants, some clever and some not, in attaining an eventual happy union.

As the works of Plautus and Terence, the pre-eminent Roman dramatists, suggest, Roman drama drew heavily upon the Greek, and followed the Greek style of dividing drama into comedies and tragedies (the satyr play completely disappeared). Although tragedy was popular in Rome, only ten tragedies have survived, all from the time of the Empire. Nine are by the stoic philosopher Seneca and the author of the other, *Octavia*, is unknown. The ornate rhetorical style and occasional gruesome scenes have led many historians to suggest that these plays were meant only for reading and never staged, but they have in fact had a respectable modern stage history and were highly influential among Renaissance tragedians. During the later years of the Roman Empire, literary drama declined, in favour of circuses, gladiatorial combats, and spectacular shows like the mock naval battles, the Naumachiae, staged in massive public spaces like the Roman Colosseum. Somewhat closer to a theatre tradition were the pantomimes, often with chorus and dancers, and the mimes, farcical comedians, who carried on something of the characters and situations of new comedy, and, some historians have argued, formed a bridge to the improvised comedy, the commedia dell'arte of the Renaissance.

Although the original stages used by Plautus and Terence appear to have been rather simple platforms with a back wall containing the doors to the houses of the various characters, much larger permanent theatres were later built throughout the Roman Empire, from Spain to the Middle East. The first of these, the largest, and the model for those that followed, was the Theatre of Pompey, built in Rome in 55 BCE, almost a century after Plautus and Terence. Although based on Greek models, the Roman theatre had distinctive features. It was free-standing, not built into a natural slope, the Greek orchestra was reduced to a semicircle, while the Hellenistic skene house was made larger and more elaborate and its projecting side wings joined to the auditorium seating so as to create a single architectural structure. These monumental buildings were found in every Roman city of any size and still today are the most distinctive features of Roman archeological sites around the Mediterranean and as far north as England.

As Christianity arose, the theatre in general, and the irreverent and salacious popular mimes in particular, were often the object of attack, but the conquests of northern invaders during the 5th century essentially put an end to theatre in the Western Empire, although wandering players are thought by many to have carried on some of its traditions through the following centuries. In the year 330 CE, however, the Emperor Constantine rebuilt the Eastern city of Byzantium and made it his capital. When Rome was captured, the eastern part of the Empire survived for another thousand years, as the Byzantine Empire. Popular classical forms like the mimes, pantomimes, and street entertainers continued into this Empire, as did great popular spectacles, such as gladiatorial combats and chariot races, but despite sustained efforts, historians have found no solid evidence of a continuing theatrical tradition, in the classical sense, in the Byzantine Empire.

Classical India

As theatre was declining in Europe, it was arising in Asia. The earliest references to dramatic representations come from India in the 2nd century BCE, and sometime between this period and the 2nd century CE the great Indian textbook on theatre, the *Natyasastra*, was created. The *Natyasastra* holds a centrality in central Asian theatre similar to that of Aristotle's *Poetics* in Europe, but it is far more extensive in scope, covering not only dramatic structure, but acting, costuming, staging, and theatre architecture. The place for performance described in the *Natyasastra* is far closer to a modern Western idea than to that of classical Greece or Rome. Exact dimensions of a normal theatre are given: a rectangular structure approximately 50 feet wide and 100 long. This area was then divided in half, one half for the audience, the other for the actors, the acting space being further divided into stage and backstage space. Unlike the great public theatres of Greece and Rome, these classical Indian theatres were sponsored by royal courts and were clearly for an elite audience, of at most about 500.

Although a variety of languages were used in these plays, the kings and divine beings spoke Sansrkit, the court language, and this tradition has come to be known as the Sanskrit theatre. About 300 Sanskrit plays survive, mostly from the 2nd and 3rd centuries CE. The plays were basically of two types, the Nataka plays, involving kings and divine beings, and the Prakarana plays, involving middle-class characters. This division suggests the division between tragedy and comedy in classical Greek drama, but there is little other similarity. Some historians have suggested that Alexander the Great, a lover of theatre, may have brought the form with him when he invaded northern India in 327 BCE, but there is no direct evidence of this, and little within the Sanskrit theatre to support it. Not only is the physical theatre totally different, but so is the drama itself. Sanskrit plays are long, with complex actions and a mixture of tonalities much more like Shakespeare than the Greeks, and invariably have happy or at least reconciled endings. The stories are mostly derived from the great Indian epics, the *Ramayana* and the *Mahabharata*.

The best known of the Sanskrit dramatists was Kalidasa, writing probably in the 4th century CE, whose *Shakuntala* has often been produced in the West. The last major Sanskrit dramatist was Bhavabhuti, in the 8th century, but the tradition continued, especially in north-east India, where the Sena court of the 11th and 12th centuries strongly supported it. Bengal subsequently became the centre of Sanskrit drama and a significant tradition continued there until the mid 19th century and the rise of the native Bengali theatre. A better-known branch of Sanskrit theatre fused with local comic performances in Kerala, south-west India, to form the Kutiyattam theatre, traditionally performed within the enclosure of Hindu temples, a form which still exists today. The all-male mimed performances last several days and feature musical accompaniment and elaborate costumes.

Classical China

Theatre developed in China almost as early as in India. The Chinese opera traces its roots to the Canjun opera of the 3rd century CE, and continued to be developed through the following centuries, primarily as a court entertainment, although the first known organized opera company in China was not formed until the early 8th century. Long before that time another major variety of world theatre had developed in China. This was the puppet theatre, often neglected by Western theatre historians. Its origins can be traced back in Asia as far as those of the live theatre. In the 1st century BCE, while the earliest Sanskrit drama was being created in India, the art of shadow puppetry was developing in China. In some parts of Asia, credit for the origin of this form goes back to the military strategist Zhang Liang, who is reported to have used large shadow puppets in the image of soldiers to defend an unguarded fortress. The first clear record of what we would today call a shadow puppet theatre, however, comes from almost a century after Zhang Liang, about 100 BCE. Then, histories of the Han dynasty speak of the sorrow of the emperor at the early death of his favourite concubine, Madame Li. To console him, an advisor promised to evoke her spirit, which he did by creating what was apparently the first shadow puppet theatre, in which a mock figure of Madam Li appeared. The king was so entranced that he encouraged the development of this art, with unhappy results. A few years later, in 96 BCE, the paranoid emperor ordered a series of investigations and executions as a result of a nightmare in which he saw himself attacked by stick-wielding puppets.

Once established, the shadow theatre gradually became an important part of Chinese culture. During the Sui and Tang dynasties (581–906), Buddhist monks and missionaries extensively employed shadow puppets to present religious instruction, and by the Song dynasty (906–1279) shadow puppetry had become a popular form of street entertainment. Travelling companies performed puppet shows in improvised theatres and the first guilds of such performers were formed. The first records of the major traditional theatre of south-east Asia, the *wayang kulit*, come from the 10th century, and although their traditional subject matter comes from the Hindu epics, many think the form itself was imported from China. Although materials differ, the theatre is essentially the same—elaborate two-dimensional figures are held up to a translucent screen illuminated from behind.

During approximately the same period that the puppet theatre was being so institutionalized, the early Chinese opera, hitherto essentially a court entertainment, began to develop popular variations. The first national troupe devoted to the performance of Chinese opera was founded by the emperor Xuanzong, who reigned from 712 to 756. This form developed steadily after this, with new varieties developing in different parts of China. The emphasis in Chinese opera remained on the music, dance, and spectacle, but song was important as well, and during the Song dynasty the earliest forms of what might be called musical dramas developed, the *nanxi* in the south and the *zaju* in the north. Both, unlike classical Chinese opera, were created for a popular audience, employed the local dialect and narratives based on a wide variety of subjects—epic, domestic, romantic, and religious. The more formal *nanxi* allowed only a single singer in each of its four acts, while the *zaju* allowed multiple characters. The *nanxi* is the older form, said to have been created during the reign of the

2. Contemporary Chinese opera

emperor Guangzong (1190–4). The *zaju* developed later, in the area around present-day Beijing. By 1280 the Mongols under Kubla Khan had completed the conquering of China and built a new city, Dadu (the ancestor of present-day Beijing), as their capital (Figure 2). Despite their warlike activities, the Mongol rulers of the new dynasty, the Yuan, strongly encouraged the theatre. The local form, the *zaju*, spread into the south as well. It developed a wider range of stock characters and more unified narrative structures, resulting in a new, Yuan form that is often called the first true theatre of China. Roughly 200 plays from this era remain. They cover a wide range of popular subjects: romances, histories, lawsuit, and bandit plays. The best-known Yuan play is surely *The Chalk Circle*, written in the later 13th century by Li Xingfu, and given new life in modern times by Bertolt Brecht's reworking of it as *The Caucasian Chalk Circle*. In the 18th century, Voltaire, in his tragedy *The Chinese Orphan*, gave similar Western exposure to another major Yuan play, *The Orphan of Zhao*, by the 13th century Yuan dramatist Ji Junxiang.

Medieval Japan

Medieval Japan was ruled by hereditary military dictators, the shoguns. Various popular entertainments, based more on dance and acrobatics than on narrative, were popular in the early years of the Shugunate, which began in 1192. One of the most popular forms was the *sangaku*, imported from China perhaps as early as the 8th century. The *sangaku* employed jugglers, acrobats, actors, and pantomimists in a form suggestive of the modern circus. In 1374, a key date in Japanese theatre history, the shogun Ashikaga Yoshimitsu witnessed a *sarugaku* company headed by the producer Kan'ami and was so impressed by their work that he became their sponsor. During the next four decades, Kan'ami and his son Zeami, supported by the court, developed, as theorists, practitioners, and playwrights, the classic Noh drama which still survives today. Zeami's *Fushikaden*, primarily devoted to the art of acting, is the foundational text of Japanese dramatic theory. The *sarugaku* performances contained both serious and comic elements, and while the Noh developed from the serious ones, the comic elements were developed into short light pieces called Kyogen. A classic performance thus might include five Noh plays separated by two Kyogen. The traditional Noh stage is derived from that of the Shinto religious dance, the *kagura*. Although constructed indoors in modern times, it retains its original outdoor configuration, an open pavilion extending into the audience, into which the actors enter over a bridge to the backstage area. The form is highly stylized, with masks, elaborate costumes, a simple background composed of a lone pine tree, a small orchestra, and a single singing narrator.

Medieval Europe

During the period of the Song dynasty, while the puppet theatre and the opera were becoming established as major theatrical forms in China and the Noh theatre was evolving in Japan, the first known post-classical dramatic works were being created in

Europe. Surprisingly, given the opposition of the Christian Church to the last classical theatre, these developed within the now-dominant Catholic culture. In the mid 10th century a Saxon nun, Hrosvitha, wrote six plays modelled on Terence, but, like Buddhist shadow plays of her Chinese contemporaries, devoted to didactic religious subjects. During this same period, sections of church ritual began to be converted into short religious plays, and a key document from England, the *Regularis Concordia*, written about 970, gave detailed instructions for the performance of such dramatic events within the church. During the following century, these liturgical plays spread throughout most of Europe, with the important exception of Spain, then a Muslim territory. Even there, theatre was apparently not absent, however. There are records of live performers in the Islamic world even before this time, and shadow puppetry, reportedly brought from China by way of Egypt, had reached Muslim Spain while the liturgical drama was spreading in the north.

At first performed within cathedrals and as part of liturgical practice, religious plays in Europe expanded and often moved out of doors. *The Mystery of Adam*, created about 1150, contains stage directions that show it was performed in open air. Until the 13th century, there is no record in medieval Europe of a secular drama, although there are ample records of travelling performers who may have presented dramatic offerings like simple farces. The French city of Arras became the first city in Europe to produce significant secular drama. Jean Bodel's 1200 religious drama, *Le Jeu de Saint Nicolas*, already contains significant secular elements, and later in the century Adam de la Halle created fully secular plays, most notably the 1283 *Le Jeu de Robin et Marion*, which also introduced music to the French secular theatre. Coincidentally, at the very time that Adam de la Halle was making major innovations in the European theatre in Arras, Ibn Daniyal, his contemporary in Cairo, was producing the most important and innovative works in the long-established Arab shadow theatre, three plays that rival or surpass those of Bodel in literary sophistication.

In 1311 a major new impetus for the development of drama, especially in England, was given by the establishment of the Corpus Christi festival, celebrating the transubstantiation. It soon became customary for the English guilds, associations of craftsmen, to present a series of biblically based plays on this occasion, the clergy having been forbidden to perform on a public stage by a papal edict of 1210. By the 1370s records show the regular performance of the groups of plays, called cycles, in a number of British towns, and during the next century they expanded across England and into Europe, becoming major civic events lasting several days and often covering the entire Christian history of the world, from the Creation to the Last Judgement.

These epic works were performed in different spaces in different countries, but all were out of doors. Sometimes they were presented on platforms arranged around town squares, as in Lucerne, Switzerland, other times a row of small stages were lined up behind a large neutral acting area, as in Valenciennes, France. The best-documented arrangements were the pageant wagons, utilized in Christian Spain and England. Each play was performed on a wagon, similar to modern parade floats, and these would either be moved to different locations in the city or be used in sequence at a single gathering point. Four complete or nearly complete cycles and parts of others survive from England, developed during the mid 14th century and performed regularly until the 1570s, when they were banned by the Protestant Queen Elizabeth due to their long association with the Catholic Church.

Renaissance theatre in Italy

While religious dramas were flourishing in northern Europe in the 15th century, the rediscovery of classical learning called the Renaissance was taking place in the Italian courts. For theatre this had major implications for both the drama and the stage. In the drama this began with the rediscovery of classical theory, most importantly Aristotle, whose writings, interpreted in various ways, has remained the bedrock of Western dramatic theory ever since. Upon readings of Aristotle and to some extent Horace, Renaissance Italian and later French theorists built the doctrine of neoclassicism, which dominated Western theatre until the early 19th century. This doctrine insisted upon the strict separation in tone, characters, subject matter, and arc of action between comedy and tragedy (although even in the Renaissance a few writers, most notably Guarini, argued for dramas of mixed tonality, which he called tragicomedies). Equally important were the so-called three unities, of time, place, and action, meaning a plot should ideally take place in a single location, within at most 24 hours, and not involve any secondary actions. Renaissance Italian dramatists looked to these instructions, and to the models of the recently rediscovered classical dramatists, in constructing their own comedies and tragedies, but in fact produced little lasting theatre. Their French successors did much better, producing, at the height of neoclassicism in the 17th century, their three greatest dramatists, Corneille, Molière, and Racine.

A quite different result of the attempt to recreate classical theatre was the invention of opera, the first example of which was *Dafne*, created by Jacopo Peri in Florence around 1597, and based on the assumption that classical theatre was a musical as well as dramatic form, with singing actors and chorus. Although of course far from actual Greek practice, the taste for opera rapidly spread, especially in the courts and among the aristocracy of 17th and 18th century Europe. In the West it has traditionally (if somewhat arbitrarily) been considered a genre separate from theatre proper, and so I will, reluctantly, not trace its developments and contributions here.

16th century Europe

The impact of the Renaissance upon the concept of the physical theatre was equally revolutionary, but even further, in fact, from actual classical practice. Most importantly, the Italian Renaissance theatre, created for the Renaissance courts, was from the beginning primarily an intimate, indoor activity, far different from the huge, open-air democratic classical performances. The first permanent theatre built during the Renaissance, the Teatro Olympico, built in 1585, attempted to recreate a small Roman stage and auditorium within an enclosed building, but it inspired no imitations. Subsequent theatres developed the familiar plan still sometimes called the 'Italianate stage', which traditionally involves an interior, rectangular space, divided between audience and performance space (essentially the same as the traditional Sanskrit theatre), and the stage elevated and framed by a proscenium arch (first used at the 1618 Teatro Farnese in Parma, Italy). Closely associated with the development of this new indoor theatre was the use of perspective scenery, derived from the keen interest of Renaissance artists in this technique. The production of the first new comedy of the Renaissance, Ariosto's *Cassario*, in 1508, utilized perspective scenery. The single-point perspective remained the basic design for proscenium theatres in Europe until around 1700, when Fernandino Galli-Bibiena, connected to two of Europe's best-known design families, introduced multiple perspectives. A century later Romanticism introduced more complex and dimensional stage arrangements, but the basic proscenium style arrangement remained and is still today the most familiar architectural form of Western theatre; during the period of European colonization, it was spread by the European colonial powers to other theatre cultures around the world, where it is now often spoken of as the 'Western' or even the 'modern' stage.

The 16th century also saw the rise in Italy of a major non-literary theatrical form, the commedia dell'arte, first recorded in 1551. This theatrical form, perhaps distantly related to late classical mimes, contained stock characters—the miserly merchant, the young lovers, the braggart soldier, the pedant—and created improvised comic plots peppered with short physically comic routines, the *lazzi*. Over the next two centuries, commedia companies travelled through much of Europe and exerted a great influence both on the visual arts and on European comic drama.

Although neoclassicism eventually exerted a strong influence in dramatic writing and staging throughout Europe, its influence was never as great in Spain and England as in Italy and France, and in the latter part of the 16th century these countries both developed major theatres that differed sharply from the neoclassical model. In England, Queen Elizabeth banned the still popular medieval religious dramas in 1568, but she enjoyed and encouraged secular drama, and during her reign England produced some of the world's most honoured dramatists. Short dramatic entertainments, called interludes, had been popular at court during Elizabeth's childhood, and in the early and middle 16th century other secular forms developed: political allegories, history plays, even a few imitations of classical comedy and tragedy.

The main line of English drama, however, did not follow the classical model, but created works that defied the unities, and though it generally kept the traditional divisions of comedy and tragedy, introduced elements of each into the other and created works that could not properly be labelled either. The outstanding example of such drama was, of course, the work of Shakespeare, but a remarkable group of other major dramatists surrounded him, headed by Christopher Marlowe, Ben Jonson, and John Webster. London had a thriving theatre culture for most of the last half of the century, but did not have a permanent public theatre until 1576 and saw almost all of its most significant dramas created in the brief period from 1590 to 1615. Public theatres on the whole were as different from those in France and Italy as were the plays. Although there were a few important indoor theatres more in the continental style, like Blackfriars, built in 1599, most were open-air structures, modelled upon the inn-yard courts that were used by players before the first theatres were built. These buildings were three storeys high, surrounding an open central court into which the stage projected so that audiences could stand on three sides of it.

A somewhat similar stage, the *corrale*, was created in Spain at the same period, based upon Spanish open courtyards surrounded by buildings. The development of Spanish theatre followed a similar trajectory to that in England, the first secular plays in the early 1500s, a professional theatre developing by mid century, and a generation of master dramatists at the turn of the next century, headed by Lope de Vega, Caldéron, and Tirso da Molina. Unlike Protestant England, however, Catholic Spain retained and developed the tradition of medieval religious drama and its major dramatists wrote both secular dramas and religious plays, called *autos sacramentales*.

The Spanish discovery and colonization of the New World meant that this century also saw the exportation into that world of European-style theatre. Shortly after Cortez conquered Mexico, Franciscan friars arrived to convert the Aztec people. One of their major tools was religious drama in the Spanish model, although they found that a rich performance culture already existed in the New World. Certain parts of this culture accorded well with the European idea of theatre, and European defenders of the sophistication of the inhabitants of the New World sometimes mentioned their theatrical gifts among their qualities. The complex cultural mixtures of dance, ritual, theatrical representation, and public ceremonies far exceeded the capacity of a European concept of theatre to describe. Indeed, such activities still challenge theatre historians today, although the strategies of performance studies have provided important new analytic tools.

As with other cultural elements, secular and religious, the theatre that developed in the wake of the conquest was in fact a *mestizo* theatre, mixing indigenous and Spanish elements. As time passed, however, the European model, as in other parts of the colonized world, came to be seen as the standard form of theatre as a cultural expression.

17th century Japan and Europe

The opening years of the 17th century, when Spanish and English drama were at their peak of achievement, saw also the appearance of one of the best-known Asian theatrical forms, the Kabuki, in Japan. This new form of dance drama was first performed in 1603 by a female performer, and remained a solely female form until 1629, when it was banned as immoral. After a brief and no more successful attempt with boy actors, the Kabuki by mid century had become a form for adult males, playing both genders, as it has remained ever since. The Kabuki entered its period of greatest flourishing in the late 17th century, but still remains a significant part of the Japanese theatre, while the Noh is today a respected but much more infrequently presented form.

The third great Japanese theatrical form appeared later in the century, in 1684, when a Kabuki playwright, Chikamatsu Monzaemon, collaborated with a professional storyteller, Takemoto Gidayu, to create a new style of puppet theatre, which became known as Bunraku. From this point on, Chikamatsu wrote primarily for the Bunraku, creating the first serious plays in Japan dealing with the merchant class. He is generally considered Japan's greatest playwright, although the great age of Bunraku was during the first half of the next century. The puppets became larger and more elaborate until after 1734 each puppet, about two-thirds life size was manipulated by three puppeteers, who carried the figure about the stage. At its height, the Bunraku theatre quite eclipsed the Kabuki, but the two forms then and after borrowed both effects and stories from each other.

During the 17th and 18th centuries, French culture, including the theatre, set the style for much of Europe. Playwrights across the continent looked to Molière and Racine as models, as in the

Renaissance they had looked to Terence and Seneca. Even the British theatre, long resistant to continental influence, shared this orientation, particularly after 1660. The Puritan triumph in the Civil Wars 20 years before had temporarily ended the monarchy and officially closed the theatres. Many leading royalists fled to France, and when king and theatre were restored in 1660, a good deal of French influence returned. The English drama of the late 17th century, dominated by the free-spirited Restoration comedy, shows this influence, but even more clear is the effect on the production of plays. For the first time women appeared on the English stage, and the open-air theatres of Shakespeare's time were not reproduced, theatre now moving definitively indoors in the continental manner.

18th century Europe

Although the 18th century in Europe did not produce dramatists of the stature of Shakespeare, Racine, or Caldéron, interest in theatre expanded in the continent and important contributions were made. In Italy, Carlo Goldoni built upon commedia dell'arte traditions to create a modern literary Italian drama. In Denmark Ludwig Holberg's comedies helped to lay the foundations of modern theatre in Scandinavia. In Germany Caroline Neuber founded a company dedicated to establishing a German literary theatre instead of the crude farces that had dominated the German stage before. The scattered German states struggled to establish a significant German theatre, a project finally realized at the end of the century by Goethe and Schiller at Weimar. The late 17th century also saw European-style theatre established on two new continents, in Australia for the cultural improvement of the British convicts deported there, and, more respectably, in the British colonies in North America, creating a new world theatre on the British model.

Another development of the later 18th century was an increased interest in moving the subject of serious theatre from the kings and heroes of the past to middle-class subjects. George Lillo anticipated this trend with his 1731 *The London Merchant*, which inspired the German Gotthold Lessing at mid century both as a theorist and dramatist. In France such leading dramatists as Voltaire, Beaumarchais, and especially Diderot produced examples of this new form, which they called the *drame*. None of these European innovators would have known that on the other side of the globe their Japanese contemporary Chikamatsu was engaged in a similar change in the subject matter of theatre, but the impetus for both was essentially the same, the decline of the old system controlled by warriors and kings and the rise of the bourgeoisie in society in general as well as in the theatre.

19th century Europe and Asia

The rise of romanticism in Europe in the early 19th century theatre effectively ended the previously dominant neoclassic system. It did not result in major changes in theatre architecture, but profoundly affected almost every other aspect of the art. Acting, scenery, and playwriting became more 'realistic', but it was on the whole a rather flamboyant and emotional realism, against which the 'realists' of the later 19th century would react. Playwrights sought situations of extreme emotion, most notably in the melodrama, a highly popular form developed at this time. Actors move from neoclassic restraint to specialize in scenes of madness and frenzy. Scenic designers left the simple classic interiors of Racine to move out into nature, presenting erupting volcanos and other spectacular phenomena.

During the romantic era Europe also saw the rise of modern nationalism, to which theatre made a major contribution. As previously subordinate linguistic and cultural communities in Europe from Albania to Norway sought to solidify their cultural identity and in many cases to go on to establish independent states, the establishment of a theatre devoted to their language and history was often a key part of the project. As European colonialism spread around the globe, it not only took with it the concept of Western theatre but also that of the theatre as an expression of national culture, an idea carried on as former colonies sought independence, with the result that national theatres, founded on the European model, can be found throughout the world today.

Around the world, countries with little theatre tradition in the European sense began to create such theatre, but often blended European methods and plays with indigenous practice and materials to create the huge variety of hybrid forms found today. Leading dramatists like Derek Walcott in Trinidad, Ola Rotimi and Wole Soyinka in Nigeria, and Sa'dallah Wannous in Syria are important representatives of this process.

Even the centuries-old theatres of Asia were not immune from this influence. In the mid 19th century wealthy citizens of Calcutta began to create private theatres in the British model and to write Western-style plays. Rabindranath Tagore, working in this tradition, become its best-known example, winning the Nobel Prize for literature in 1913. The forcible opening of Japan to the West by Perry in the 1850s involved not only trade but culture. In the 1880s an East–West hybrid theatre, the *shinpa*, developed, which somewhat resembled Western melodrama but with distinct kabuki elements. A decade later Soyo Tsubouchi introduced the *shingeki* (new theatre), directly drawn from Western models, especially Shakespeare. At the beginning of the new century, these Western theatre models were exported to Korea and China, where again they became the basis of modern theatre in the far East.

In mid 19th century Europe, the exuberant romantic drama gave way to more subdued and realistic drama of every-day life, as can be seen in the so-called 'cup-and-saucer' plays of Tom Robertson in 1860s England. Domestic realism was taken to new depths in the 1880s with the works of Henrik Ibsen, which are generally considered to initiate modern theatre in the West, and thanks to

Western global influence he was known even as far away as Japan by the 1890s and his plays presented around the world in the early years of the new century. These helped to solidify the domestic middle-class drama, performed in realistic style in domestic settings, as the standard Western theatre form, which indeed it remains today, especially in the United States.

The 20th century

Many of the major Western dramatists of the next century, among them Anton Chekhov, Bernard Shaw, and Arthur Miller, worked in this form, but despite its dominance Ibsenesque realism was almost immediately challenged by non-realistic forms. The most important of these in Europe were symbolism at the turn of the century, expressionism during and after the First World War, both inspired in part by the works of Ibsen's major contemporary, August Strindberg in Sweden, the epic theatre of Bertolt Brecht, and the theatre of the absurd, led by French dramatists Eugene Ionesco and Samuel Beckett. Another important counter-force to modern Western realism was the search in many former European colonies for indigenous theatre forms to blend with or counteract this dominant European style.

Each of these challenges to realism brought with it stage designs that sharply departed from Ibsen's realistic living rooms, but the staging of even Ibsen underwent a radical change in the 20th century with the rise of the director. At least since Max Reinhardt, at the opening of the 20th century, modern directors, except in England and the United States, have experimented widely with the interpretations and visual styles of their plays, so that the dominant figure in the modern European theatre is no longer the actor or the playwright but the director.

Moreover by the late 20th century as theatre became international, leading directors like Peter Brook, Robert Wilson, Ong Keng Sen, Peter Stein, Giorgio Strehler and Tadashi Suzuki became as well known around the world as in their native countries. They have developed no international style however, each reflecting the hybridity of modern world theatre by combining local and global materials in unique ways. All, for example, have presented major Shakespeare works, but in styles so totally different that any informed viewer could easily distinguish them.

Actors and companies have travelled about for centuries, but only in the late 20th century, thanks to ever-increasing ease of communication and travel for both audiences and performers, did theatre become truly international. This internationalism and hybridity extended from great international festivals, like Avignon and Edinburgh, which presented theatre artists from around the world, to the work of individual companies, like that of Peter Brook, whose International Centre for Theatre Research gathers actors from multiple traditions, sharing no common language, training or concept of theatre, to create works in a new, hopefully more global style.

Theatre and life

Despite the enormous range of production styles and visual approaches of the modern theatre, the great majority of such theatre still takes place in some variation of the traditional European proscenium stage. Many alternatives to such staging however have developed in recent times. Early 20th century directors, especially in Russia and Germany, experimented with different actor–audience arrangements, leading in the next century to theatres in the round, thrust stages, projecting out into the audience, and the mixing of actor–audience spaces utilized in Poland by Jerzy Grotowski and characterized by Richard Schechner as 'environmental theatre'. Nikolai Evreinov, in Revolutionary Russia, presciently advocated the blurring of the boundaries between theatre and life and in his 1920 reconstruction of the Storming of the Winter Palace on its actual location anticipated both the battle re-enactments and the site-specific theatre experiments of the later 20th century, both of which challenged the traditional concept of theatre and its traditional concept of space. Peter Brook's often-quoted beginning to his book, *The Empty Space* summarizes this new attitude: 'I can take any empty space and call it a bare stage.'

Normal site-specific performances still separated audience and performance in a fairly traditional way, and although environmental theatre did away with that formal arrangement, it still kept audience and actor spaces fairly distinct. This spatial distinction began to dissolve with promenade performances in England and elsewhere, where the audience had no fixed space, but needed to move about to watch the performance. A further dissolving of this traditional boundary has occurred in the 21st century with the rise of what has become widely known in England and the United States as immersive theatre, in which the actors and audience share a common space and common objects. In more radical versions of this form, audiences are encouraged to interact with the performers and even to co-create the performance with them.

This blurring of art and life began to appear in a somewhat different form at the end of the century when artists began to apply to theatre the strategies of 'readymades'. Just as Marcel Duchamp famously converted a urinal into an art object by signing and displaying it, artists presented real life as 'theatre' by asking audiences to view it as such. This theatrical 'framing' could be literal, as when Robert Whitman in 1967 seated an audience in a warehouse with an open loading door and drew its curtains to reveal the activity on the street outside as 'theatre'. Or, more commonly, it could be simply situational, as when Reza Abdoh mixed actors and street scenes in New York's meatpacking district in 1990, when the Foundry theatre created similar mixtures in 2009 for an audience touring New York's South Bronx in a chartered bus, or in a variety of productions by Berlin's Rimini Protokoll which have sent audience members out into such mixed environments guided by cell phones. At the beginning of the 20th century, Evreinov urged audiences to view the world as a theatre. A century later an important part of experimental work is engaged in testing that project.

While Peter Brook took the theatre out of its traditional architecture, both in Europe and Asia, and claimed that any 'empty space' could be claimed as a theatre, simply by calling it a stage, this experimental work goes a step further, by taking space that is not empty, but already filled with human activity, and making it into a theatre simply by calling it so. This is not simply an expansion of Brook's idea, but a change in what art is. For Brook, the empty space in fact becomes a theatre when he as an artist creates a theatrical work in it. For Evreinov and for Rimini Protokoll, any space, empty or not, can become a theatre if audiences can be convinced to experience it as such. If we hold to the traditional, artist-oriented point of view, the question 'what is theatre?' can be answered by considering, as most of this essay has done, the different artistic and social assumptions within which theatre artists have created their work. If we focus instead upon reception, the answer to 'what is theatre?' changes, and becomes whatever an audience can be convinced to see as theatre. The rise of performance studies, which will be discussed in a later chapter, in its attention to theatrical elements of everyday life, has provided further impetus for this expansion of a theatrical consciousness. Theatre is no longer an isolated art form, confined within a particular building, performed by a particular group of people in a particular style and following particular rules, but has become inextricably intertwined with human social activity in general.

Chapter 2
Religion and theatre

There is scarcely a religion in the world that does not have close connections with theatre. Often in the West these have been considered closely related but separate human activities, both involving consciously repeated words and actions, but one sacred, involving direct communication with the divine, the other secular, with traditionally presented enacted narratives. From this distinction has come the endless and basically futile debate over which came first. In modern times, thanks to the influence of a group of English classicists at the beginning of the 20th century called the Cambridge ritualists, the general opinion in the West has been that ritual observance came first, and that theatre developed only later, when the forms remained after the faith was lost. Theatre, in effect, was seen as a kind of dead ritual. This distinction is still generally maintained in the West, even though the rise of performance studies has brought ritual and theatre together as parallel objects of study. At other times, and even more in other parts of the world, this modern Western division has often been almost non-existent.

Given the enormous complexity and possible variation of both theatre and religion, both in turn divided into countless varied forms, anything like an overview of their relationships would be an almost impossible task, but this essay will attempt to lay out some general patterns and contrasts, and suggest some of the historical and geographical implications of this relationship. Doubtless it will be best to start with the Western theatre, as this is the tradition likely most familiar to readers of this text. The most important thing to note about theatre and religion in the West is that all three of the great Western religions—Judaism, Christianity, and Islam—have a common root in belief in a single God and a common religious foundational law, set out in the first five books of the Bible, sometimes called the Books of Moses. This has had a profound effect on the relationship of Western religion to theatre. The condemnation of images, fundamental to Mosaic law, has encouraged a deep suspicion of any form of mimesis, especially involving the body. This suspicion of mimesis is philosophically close to that of the pagan Plato, who also saw any such activity as distracting from the essential and unitary good. It is often reported that Islam never developed a theatre because Mohammed condemned representations of the human body. Although this is not in fact true, it certainly is true that among the more conservative Islamic scholars, as among conservative Jewish and Christian ones, the theatre has always been viewed with deep distrust and often specifically condemned. Often these condemnations have been linked also to the theatre's connection with the body, and thus with bodily sins, especially sexual ones, but from a philosophical point of view, the fear of mimetic duplication is more fundamental.

Early Christianity and the theatre

In fact, in each of these religions there is a substantial tradition of specifically religious drama well before modern times. Somewhat surprisingly, the first known Biblical drama, preserved only in fragments, was the creation of Jewish dramatist, Ezekial, who created a tragedy in Greek about Moses in the 2nd century BCE. In the Hellenistic and the later Roman Empire, as the theatre became both more associated with an oppressive rule, more decadent, and more dedicated to the suppression of such religious minorities as Christians and Jews, the fathers of both religions condemned the theatre and its works as creations of the devil.

Ironically, in the late Middle Ages, when a literary theatre tradition re-emerged in Europe, it was within the Christian Church, where parts of the liturgy began to be enacted on special occasions, creating an atmosphere in which an amazing variety of theatre was developed. The earliest known such enactment was the *Quem Quaeritis*, *c*.925, a short Resurrection play. The first known medieval European dramatist was a northern German nun, Hrosvitha, who created six religious plays modelled on Terence later in this century. During the following century liturgy-based theatre spread through much of Europe except Muslim-occupied Spain. First performed inside churches and monasteries by priests and monks, during the 12th century the plays moved out into public spaces, and became large productions involving entire communities, but still maintaining their Biblical subject matter. In England, groups of such plays, called mysteries, were performed in series called cycles, and by the end of the 15th century, cycle performances were offered in several parts of Europe on festival days. In some places the cycle, which might cover only the life of Christ, or the entire story of the Bible, would be performed on different small stages, called mansions, around a central playing area. In England separate plays were often performed on wagons, called pageants, which would move in sequence about a city. Despite their great popularity, the cycles were viewed by Queen Elizabeth as too closely tied to Catholicism, and after the Church of England broke with Rome in 1534 such religious drama was banned in England (Figure 3).

Although the mystery plays are the best-known and most widely spread European religious drama in the late Middle Ages, they were supplemented by other popular forms of such drama, most importantly the miracle or saints' plays and the moralities. The miracle plays were based not on the Bible but on the lives and legends of the Christian saints and martyrs. Most of the preserved

3. Modern reconstruction of a medieval performance in Coventry, England

examples of this genre come from France, headed by Jean Bodel's *Jeu de Saint Nicolas*, from the end of the 12th century. The moralities developed around 1400 and continued to flourish until the middle of the following century. They did not deal with traditional characters, but with abstract qualities treated in a dramatic fashion. *Everyman*, the best-known medieval drama, is the outstanding example of such work.

Early Jewish and Islamic theatre

Theatre within the medieval Jewish community did not develop so widely or in so many varieties, but it appeared almost as early. The

Purimspiel, a folk performance based on the Book of Esther, was well established during the 12th century and by the 16th century had become a widespead carnival play that has been performed ever since. During the next century, like the British cycle plays, it inspired other similar plays on other Biblical stories, like the sale of Joseph by his brothers, or David's slaying of Goliath, and produced the first significant Hebrew dramatist of Europe, Yehuda Sommo (Leone de'Sommi) of Mantua. Himself a playwright, actor, director, and theatre theorist, de'Sommi argued that the Jews and not the Greeks had invented the drama, citing the Book of Job as an example.

Although Islam is widely considered inimical to theatrical performance by Western scholars, there in fact exists a long-established tradition of religious drama within Islam that bears many striking resemblances to the cycle dramas of Europe. This is the Ta'zieh of Iran. Elegaic musical dramas mourning the death of heroes were performed in Persia before the coming of Islam in the 7th century and are thought to have helped lay the groundwork for the Ta'zieh, one of the world's great religious dramas. The origins of the Islamic form have been traced to the 10th century, but it was not until Shi'ism replaced the previously dominant Sunni Islam in Persia at the beginning of the 16th century that the Ta'zieh, closely connected with Shi'ism, could flourish. These two varieties of Islam go back to almost the origins of the faith, growing from a schism over the question of succession after the death of Muhammad. In the early years of the schism the Shia champion Hussein was killed at the battle of Kerbala, and his death has been a central day of mourning for Shia Muslims ever since. As these mourning celebrations became more elaborate, they gradually evolved into a series of short plays, showing events surrounding the fatal battle and all manner of related materials, presented in cycles of dramas very similar in structure to the cycle plays of England, but with the martyrdom of Hussein instead of the Passion of Christ at their centre. Although the Ta'zieh had its greatest flourishing in the 18th century, it is still performed in Shi'ia communities around the world.

Early Hindu and Buddhist theatre

Thus we see that even with the deep suspicion of theatre as a mimetic art among conservative elements of the Western monotheistic religions, all developed significant theatrical traditions with close ties to religious celebrations and ceremonies. Generally speaking, non-Western performance has been tied to religious practice from the very beginning and the tensions found in Christianity, Islam, and Judaism really have no parallels in the non-Western world. In the East, as in the West, the earliest traces of theatre are found in religious practice, in this case in the subcontinent of India, where theatre from its beginnings was intertwined with the two major religions of the subcontinent at the start of the common era, Hinduism and Buddhism. Buddhism appeared in the 6th century BCE, based on the teachings of its founder, Siddhartha Gautama. Hinduism, though its roots go back much further, was developed some five centuries later, as Buddhism was beginning to decline. During the century just before and after the founding of Christianity in the West, both of these religions developed major dramatic traditions, created in the common Sanskrit language.

Hindu mythology provides a more prominent justification for theatre than any of the other major religions of the world. After the four Vedas, the foundational texts for Hindu religion and culture, were created, Indra, the king of the Gods, was said to have approached Brahma, the creator, and requested an entertainment to make more joyous the existence of gods and men. Brahma then took elements from each of the four existing Vedas—dance, song, mimicry, and passion—and combined them to make a fifth Veda, the theatre. The celestial architect Vishwakarma was summoned to construct a celestial stage and the sage Bharata was appointed as the conductor of these heavenly performances. Bharata, a half-mythological figure, is said to be the creator of the first great treatise on Indian dramaturgy, the *Natyasastra*. Its date of composition is debated, but it was probably after 140 BCE when

Patañjali, a Hindu master of Yoga, created the *Mahābhāsya*, one of the great classics of Sanskrit grammar, which contains the earliest known reference to drama in India, and indeed in Asia.

Although classical Indian drama is most closely associated with Sanskrit, the oldest Indian dramas, the *sanvâdas*, were in fact created in the more lower-class language of Prâkrit, a form so closely associated with the theatre in the 1st and 2nd centuries BCE and CE that several of its dialectics have been characterized as the 'dramatic Prâkrits'. They drew upon the same mythological base as did the later Sanskrit drama, the stories of the *Mahabharata* and the *Ramayana*, whose relation to these dramas was very similar to that of the Bible to the mystery plays of the Western Middle Ages. Indeed, the earliest of these *sanvâdas* reportedly featured Krisna or Shiva acting and dancing the leading role, and the narratives were often drawn from the eventful lives of these deities. Later, as the so-called Sanskrit theatre developed, it often utilized a blend of languages: gods and the nobility spoke Sanskrit and characters of the lower social classes Prâkrit.

Despite theatre's mythic roots in Hinduism, the earliest masters of the art came from both Hinduism and Buddhism. The Buddhist philosopher-poet Aśvaghosa created his *Satiputra-prakana* in the 1st century CE, reflecting Buddhist concerns within this common classical and literary language. At roughly the same time, the first major Hindu Sanskrit dramas were being created by Bhasa and King Sudraka. The Hindu tradition and Hindu subject matter dominated this form, however, culminating in the major poet Kalidasa, thought to have been a Brahmin priest, in the late 4th century CE. His most famous work, *Shakuntala*, is based, like much Sanskrit drama, on a story from one of the Hindu epics, in this case the *Mahabharata*.

The growing dominance of Islam in India from the 11th century onward is often cited as a cause of the decline or even disappearance of theatre in the subcontinent, but this is, in fact, true neither of theatre in general nor of religious theatre in particular. For one thing, the Hindu theatre itself continued in southern India and elements of it are still preserved in the dance dramas of that region. For another, Islam was by no means the negative force in terms of theatre as it is seen in much Western thought. The Islamic passion plays of Persia spread into the subcontinent and are still performed today in Islamic communities there. For another, Hindu religious drama, like the religion itself, spread on into south-east Asia, where it received a surprising reinforcement from Islam, in the form of the work of Sufi missionaries, instrumental in spreading their concept of Islam east into Asia and south into Africa.

Sufi missionaries, like missionaries in other times and places, utilized theatre as a method of spreading knowledge of their faith to other peoples. This process was particularly interesting in south-east Asia, where the Sufi missionaries took Hindu dramatizations from the *Ramayana* and reworked them with Islamic material. This tradition was most significantly developed in the puppet theatre, such as the Indonesian *wayang*, which appeared as early as the 10th century, presenting stories from the Hindu epics. Thus in many parts of south-east Asia, theatre was introduced as a practice grounded in religion but combining Hindu and Islamic material. Meanwhile in India itself, the *Ramayana* became available to a wide public in the 17th century, inspiring dramatic re-enactment in the Ramilla, beginning about 1625. Variations of this multi-day epic are today performed not only in India, but in Hindi diasporic communities around the world, especially in Africa and south-east Asia.

Buddhist theatre in China and Japan

Although Buddhism was in decline in the land of its birth even before the arrival of Islam, it had spread and was flourishing elsewhere, particularly in south-east Asia, where its influence upon the development of theatre was very great, and in China, which became the religion's major home. Despite this, however,

China never developed a significant Buddhist theatre tradition. Buddhist-influenced theatre first appeared in south-east Asia in what is now Burma, then spread to what is now Thailand. The earliest known theatre in this area, the *nora*, developed during the 14th century from a blending of Buddhist and local animist elements. The earliest *nora* narrative tells of a bird-woman who becomes a prince's wife after her wings are stolen. The story is found in many cultures but entered south-east Asia as one of the popular *Jataka* tales, dealing with previous lives of the Buddha. For Buddhist dramatists, the *Jataka* tales served as religious source material parallel to the *Ramayna* and the *Mahabharata*. The *nora* remained a popular form of theatre in Burma and Thailand until the 18th century, and is indeed still occasionally performed there today.

In China, early Buddhist performance took the form of ritual dance, and a particularly important form of such performance, the *ennen*, or longevity dance, was developed during the 8th century, flourished until the 16th century, and is still performed in a few temples in Japan today. Traditionally, it was performed by priests and followed the ceremonial reading of religious texts, the sutras, in Buddhist temples. Although the *ennen* and similar performances did not play a major role in the development of the classical Chinese theatre, when exported to Japan they proved far more influential. Seami, who first articulated and theorized the best-known classical dramatic form of Asia, the Japanese Noh, traced its origins directly back to the Buddhist *ennen*. Actual *ennen* dances are found in a few Noh dramas, but the Noh itself is deeply infused with Noh philosophy and principles. Like the other great world religions, Buddhism has developed in many forms and variations. In medieval Japan, it was Zen Buddhism that was generally favoured by artists and patrons of art, following the model of the painters and poets of the Sung dynasty in China, but Zeami drew not only upon Zen for inspiration but also on the more popular Amidist Buddhism, which saw Buddha as a god-like figure ruling over a Western Land of paradise.

Although Buddhism has clearly left its mark on the content of the Noh dramas, perhaps especially in their focus on the vanity and transitory nature of life, native Japanese shamanism and Shinto also made important contributions to both the form and the staging. Seami himself noted that traditional Shinto ritual dances were part of the inspiration for the Noh. The most important of these, performed in Japan since the 7th century, was the *kagura*, celebrating the emergence of the sun goddess Amaterasu from the darkness of a cave. *Okina*, the oldest play in the Noh repertory, is in fact essentially a Shinto ritual, and the classic Noh stage with its back wall containing a painted pine tree is modelled on a Shinto shrine.

The next major theatrical form to appear in Japan, the Kabuki, retained distinct Buddhist elements, but turned toward the secular. Kabuki was created by a Buddhist temple assistant, Izumo no Okuni, in 1605, when she was sent to Kyoto to perform sacred dances to raise money for the major shrine of Izumo. Although her dances had a religious base, Okuni introduced folk elements and sexual innuendo, with great success. Her all-female company became so closely associated with sexual licence that the government banned companies first of women, then of young men, before finally establishing the mature male form, which remained in place from the early 17th century onward. In this more mature form Kabuki reflected more closely the religious background of the classical Japanese stage, drawing heavily, as did Noh, on the transitoriness of the world, and upon Confucianism for an emphasis upon personal duty.

In south-east Asia, the European Renaissance and Baroque periods saw a flourishing and proliferation of the traditional Wayang, which had been an important part of Indonesian culture and dedicated to Islamic and Hindu religious material for centuries. In the 15th century, the Topeng dance, featuring live actors, appeared in Bali and Java. Two centuries later, the Balinese court developed a related theatre, the Wayang Wong. Though these both utilized human performers, another 17th century puppet form, the Wayang Golek, was developed in West Java. Although very different in style, these and many other variations all trace their origins to the Wayang Kulit, and all retained and still retain today their religious, predominantly Hindu, orientation. Several forms, especially the Wayang Golek, have also strong Muslim connections, and as recently as the 1960s a Jesuit priest, Brother Timotheus Wignyosubroto, created 'revelation Wayangs' for religious instruction in Java in the centuries-old missionary tradition.

The tradition of religious theatre in Spain and Portugal

At almost the same time that the new form of Kabuki was presenting a more secular alternative to the strongly religious-based Noh, the European theatre was in the full flower of its even more secular Renaissance. The religious drama that was found throughout the Christian world during the Middle Ages could still be seen here and there until into the 18th century, but in most of Europe drama of this sort was clearly disappearing by the late 16th century. The most significant exceptions to this were Spain and Portugal. During the Middle Ages all but part of northern Spain was Islamic, but the Spanish Christian kingdoms produced religious drama similar to that already discussed in most of Europe. By the time the Islamic Moors were expelled from Spain and Portugal, in the late 15th century, the peak of the great medieval religious dramas had passed, but religious concerns continued to remain central to the Spanish and Portuguese theatre when most of the theatres in the rest of Europe were turning, during the Renaissance, to more secular concerns. It is significant that the claimed founders of both the Spanish and the Portuguese theatre, Juan del Encina, Lope de Rueda, and Gil Vicente, began their careers as writers of religious drama. All later produced secular works as well, but Vicente, who became as prominent in Portuguese drama as Caldéron in Spain, continued, like Caldéron, to be a major creator of religious drama throughout his career.

With the consolidation of the Spanish and Portuguese states came also a consolidation of Catholicism in these nations during the 16th and 17th centuries. During this time most of Europe was embroiled in the struggle between Catholicism and Protestantism, and theatre, already challenged by Renaissance humanism, was further damaged by its long association with the Catholic Church. Only in Spain and Portugal, where Catholicism reigned unchallenged, did a thriving religious drama continue to exist alongside the more typical Renaissance secular theatre. The leading Spanish and Portuguese dramatists of the Renaissance all contributed to the tradition of *autos sacramentales* (sacred plays). The prolific Lope de Vega is said to have created over 400 such works and his less prolific but perhaps even more distinguished contemporary Caldéron more than 70. The first of Vicente's many *autos*, created in 1510, actually bore the ominous name *Auto de fé* (literally 'act of faith'), with a plot similar to the almost contemporary northern European morality play *Everyman*, an allegorical depiction of Everyman's journey towards death and redemption. The fact that this same phrase was applied in Spain to the public trials and burnings of heretics suggests the close cultural connection that existed between the two as religious cultural performances.

The first public theatres, built at this time in both Spain and England, clearly reflected the different relationship between theatre and religion. London playhouses like the Fortune or the Globe were commercial enterprises, erected to make money for their companies. The two public theatres in Madrid, called *corrales*, were erected by religious charities and the profits gained from them were devoted to the charitable work of these brotherhoods. The plays continued to be a major part of Spanish culture until they were banned by royal decree in 1765, due to their growing vulgarity and the protests of secular students of the Enlightenment.

Religious theatre and colonialism

The fact that the first two great modern colonial powers, Spain and Portugal, were also monolithically Catholic, meant that the spreading of the Catholic faith was central to their colonization of the New World. This process began early in the 16th century with Cortez's conquest of Mexico. When Cortez landed in Mexico in 1519, he made common cause with the rulers of Tlaxcala, already in combat with the Aztecs. The first Franciscan monks, dedicated to bringing religion and European culture to the New World, arrived in Tlaxcala in 1524 and seeing what they considered distinct theatrical elements in the ritual dramas and public celebrations of the native people, seized upon theatrical performance as the most efficacious and non-violent strategy of enlightenment and conversion. Religious drama thus became central to the Spanish colonial project from the 1520s onwards. One of the Franciscans who arrived in 1524 assumed the name Motolinía ('the poor one' in the native language Nahuatl) and provided invaluable records of New Spain in the mid 16th century. Apparently the first European-style play presented in the New World set the tone for such drama. It portrayed the Last Judgement and was created by the first bishop appointed to New Spain, the Franciscan Andrés de Olmos, in 1533.

In his 1541 *Historia de los Indios de Nueve España*, Motolinía provides a detailed description of elaborate Christian religious festivals held in Tlaxcala in 1538 and 1539, including elaborate processions, four *autos sacramentales* in the Nahuatl language, and a dramatic spectacle also in Nahuatl, *The Conquest of Jerusalem*, which depicted the victory of the Christians over the Moors in the taking of the Holy City. The Moors were played by indigenous actors, who as defeated Moors were baptized at the end of the play. Since the actors were in fact not baptized before, the production became a remarkable representation of the merging of theatre and the real dynamics of the conquest.

Eleven 16th century Nahuatl *autos* from Mexico have been preserved, but there were doubtless many more. Although their structure and subject matter were derived from the *autos* in contemporary Spain, the Franciscans used not only the indigenous language but whenever possible indigenous references and performance practices to make their message as accessible as possible to its audience. Hence the first post-conquest drama of the New World was from the beginning a mixed form, but its foundations on both sides were primarily religious. A corrale in the Spanish style was created for the presentation of these new dramas in Mexico City in 1597, less than 20 years after the first corrale in Madrid. The plays presented here showed much the same range as those in Madrid (and indeed were in many cases the same plays), a mixture of the religious *autos sacramentales* and the more secular *comedias*. Religious drama remained a significant part of the repertoire through the following century, however, reaching its fullest expression in the three *autos* of the Mexican nun, Sor Juana Ines de la Cruz, published in 1692.

Another major source of post-Conquest religious drama was the Jesuits, who arrived somewhat later, in 1572, and who rivalled the Franciscans in their dedication to religious instruction through drama. It has been estimated that in Mexico City alone some 52 religious dramas were performed in Jesuit schools between 1575 and 1600. In Peru the Jesuits, who arrived in 1568, were even more active than the Franciscans in the production of religious drama. A public corrale was erected in Lima not long after Mexico City, in 1605. In Peru the Jesuits created hybrid linguistic and cultural dramas, as did the Franciscans, mixing Spanish and Quechan elements, but in Mexico their productions were almost entirely not in the indigenous language, but in Latin. This followed the pattern that had already been well established in Jesuit institutions in Europe, which from the beginning had a strong interest in the theatre, not so much for conversion as for the instruction of both viewers and performers. Central as the theatre was for Spanish Franciscans as part of their missionary project in the New World, it was not a form in which the order showed much interest otherwise. The situation was very different with the Jesuits, especially in the 16th and 17th centuries, when the production of religious drama was a central concern.

The Jesuit order was founded in 1534 and just 14 years later, in 1548, established the first Jesuit school, in Messina, Italy, beginning a commitment to education that the order would eventually take around the world. The Messina school produced its first drama only three years later, and it became customary here, as in later Jesuit schools, to present at least two religious dramas in Latin each year. Within the next 100 years some 500 Jesuit colleges were established over much of the European continent, and it has been estimated they presented at least 100,000 plays between 1650 and 1700. The fact that this vast amount of religious drama, a significant portion of the European dramatic output in this century, has gone largely unremarked and unstudied by most theatre historians, indicates the hold that the narrative of a largely secular modern European theatre has upon the field. These were by no means restricted only to small and select student audiences. Members of the aristocracy and nobility frequently attended and the plays were also presented at major public festivals, sometimes, especially in Vienna, drawing audiences numbering into the thousands.

The New World theatrical activities of the other major early colonial power, Portugal, were less extensive than those of Spain, but very similar in execution. The key figure in pioneering these activities in Brazil was one of the first Jesuit missionaries, José de Anchieta Llarena, trained in one of the first Jesuit Colleges, at Coimbra in Portugal, and arriving in Brazil with the first Jesuit missionaries in 1553. For most of the rest of the century he worked with the indigenous people, the Tupi. He studied and eventually wrote in the Tupi language, and combined it with Latin, Spanish, and Portuguese in the many dramas he produced, strongly influenced by the Vicente tradition, both religious and secular.

Jesuit missionaries also took European religious drama to south Asia. Saint Francis Xavier founded a Jesuit college in the Portuguese colony of Goa, on the east Indian coast, in 1542, and began soon after to produce religious drama there. The Jesuits expanded these activities into Sri Lanka, to the south of India, soon after their arrival there in 1602. A century later these plays, still popular, were supplemented by a passion play created by Brother Jacome Goncalvez, which was an unusual variation of puppet theatre, with statues moved about by manipulators beneath the carpet on which they stood. This unusual form remained popular in Sri Lanka until the early 19th century, when live actors replaced the statues.

Baroque religious theatre in Europe

Although the international and influential Jesuit drama of the 16th through 18th centuries has been given little attention by most theatre historians, the religious drama of the Protestant Reformation has received even less, although in central Europe, especially in Germany, it was for the rest of this century a dominant part of the theatre offerings. With the express blessing and encouragement of Martin Luther, Protestant authors from the beginnings of the Reformation created religious, primarily biblical, plays, both for moral instruction and to improve the individual knowledge of the Bible so important to the Protestant project. In England, however, religious drama had been recently enough banned to still be associated with Catholicism, and the Puritans, who came to power in the 1640s, deposing the king, saw theatre as immoral as well. During their control of the state, lasting until 1660, the Protestant parliament closed all theatres and sought to abolish theatre in England.

Luther shared the British Protestant suspicion of the passion plays, focused on the life of Christ, but he felt less concerned about dramatic representations based on the Old Testament, and these became the focus of central European Protestant religious drama. The story of Joseph was especially favoured, and was the subject of the first major drama in this new tradition, created in 1635 in the Netherlands by, somewhat ironically, a Jesuit priest, Cornelius Crocus. Countless Protestant dramatists followed Crocus during the next century, with Joseph, Susanna, and Judith being particularly popular subjects. These productions soon moved out of the schools and into public venues where some expanded to rival the most elaborate of the medieval cycle plays, lasting several days with casts in the hundreds and audiences in the thousands. Hans Sachs, primarily remembered today as the author of popular farces, is said to have turned over half of the Bible into religious plays, of which he wrote over 150.

The first known drama in the Slavic nations was liturgical, apparently imported from Byzantium sometime before the 16th century. Particularly popular was the 'Furnace Play', based on the Biblical story of Nebuchadnezzar and the Hebrew children. The conservative Orthodox Church claimed that the Furnace Plays were really part of the liturgy and not actual theatre, like religious plays in the West, but it is hardly a coincidence that the first work claimed as a drama in Russia was *On Nebuchadnezzar the King*, by Symeon Polotsk. Clearly Symeon, a Jesuit priest who served as court poet toward the end of the 17th century, simply created a Jesuit school drama out of this popular story His contemporary, Gregory in Moscow, also offered works on such favoured Jesuit subjects as Esther, Tobias, and Judith.

During the 17th century, when the French theatre assumed a dominence in Europe that would not be challenged until the rise of Romanticism, the theatre, though strongly influenced by Greek models and subjects, remained largely secular. The Catholic Church, which had largely separated itself from the theatre at the

end of the Middle Ages, remained in France generally opposed
to this art and to anyone associated with it. In 1641 Louis XIV
extended legal rights to French actors, but the French Church
continued to deny them all sacraments, from baptism to last rites.
Molière's career-long struggle with the Church is well known.

Even in this unfriendly environment, however, a significant body
of religious drama was produced by the central French dramatist
of the period, Jean Racine. Racine was trained at a school
established by the Jansenists, a strict Catholic reform movement,
and although his mentors, opposed to theatre, condemned him
for his choice to become a dramatist, critics have generally agreed
that his studies of the evil effects of human passions are deeply
infused with Jansenist thought, even thought the subjects are
from the Greek and Roman classics, rather as the classic Noh
dramas are profoundly influenced by Buddhism, even when their
subjects are drawn from other sources. Even more strikingly,
Racine in his final years, when he had turned away from
playwriting to become the royal historiographer, created two late
plays, both drawn from Biblical sources. They were created at the
request of the queen, for performance by the girls at Saint-Cyr, a
convent school under her patronage. The first, *Esther* (1689),
drew upon the same source as countless Purim plays in the
Jewish tradition, but the second, *Athalie* (1691), told of a much
more obscure queen, from the book of Second Kings, but one
whose fatal passions fitted more closely with those of the central
figures in the dramatist's earlier work.

Religious theatre in the 18th century

The 18th century saw less specifically religious theatre in
Europe than any previous historical period. The Catholic
Church maintained its conservative opposition, calling in 1777
upon the elector of Bavaria, where medieval passion dramas
were still popular, to ban them. On the other hand, the thinkers
of the Enlightenment in general found the mysticism of religion

incompatible with their devotion to reason, and even the relatively rare plays created by these thinkers that had an apparently religious subject were generally either designed to condemn traditional religion, like Voltaire's 1741 *Fanaticism or Mahomet the Prophet*, or were broad humanist statements that subsumed all religions in a genteel Enlightenment benevolence, like Lessing's 1779 *Nathan the Wise*. Even in Spain, the long-dominant *autos sacramentales* were banned by royal edict in 1765, though they continued to be performed in smaller towns and in the New World. In fact, in Mexico and elsewhere they never disappeared, and especially in the form of shepherd and nativity plays may still be seen today.

In Japan, one could argue for a parallel rise in non-religious theatre, with the growing popularity of the more secular Kabuki and the subsequent puppet theatre, the Bunraku, but the Noh continued both its significant position and its clear religiosity. Elsewhere in Asia, religion and theatre remained closely intertwined. In south-east Asia, Buddhist, Hindu, and even some Muslim elements remained at the centre of the various dance dramas and puppet theatres that were the major theatre activities in these areas. This century also saw the rise of the Persian passion play, the Ta'zieh, which was cited earlier as the most significant example of Islamic religious drama. The greatest flourishing of this religious cycle was during the late 18th and early 19th centuries, although it continued to be popular enough to inspire the building of its largest theatre, the Takia-ye Dawlat in Tehran in 1876. Seating more than 4,000 spectators, it was considered by many even more elaborate and elegant than the great opera houses of Europe, then at the peak of their architectural extravagance. Although the Ta'zieh was structurally similar, as many historians have noted, to the medieval European cycle plays, its development several centuries later meant that it flourished at a time when major religious drama had been pushed from European stages by the combined forces of the Enlightenment and the rise of positivism and scientism in the 19th century. Although centred in Iran, the Ta'zieh spread into India, the Gulf

States, and eventually even to the Caribbean, in all of which places it is still performed today.

Religious theatre and post-colonialism

Globally speaking, however, theatre and religion reached their point of greatest separation during the 19th century, when the European colonialism begun in the 15th century reached its zenith and extended to every part of the world. From the Spanish Conquest onward the exportation of European theatre was a significant part of the colonial project, but with Europe's turn toward secularism, the theatre exported in the 19th century was seen not as a tool of religious conversion but as a tool for instructing the colonized in the ideals of the secular enlightenment. The priests of the 15th century exported the *autos sacramentales* of Caldéron, the educators of the 19th century the social dramas of Ibsen.

As the colonialist era faded, however, this very secularism spawned a new interest in religious theatre, widely seen in the postcolonial world as an indigenous form suppressed by the colonialists and important to be recovered as a part of a new search for cultural identity. Doubtless the best-known example of this dynamic is the work of Nigerian dramatist Wole Soyinka, who has continually drawn upon Yoruban religious material for the themes and structures of his plays. Nigeria has been a centre of such work, but similar examples abound in post-colonial theatre. In India Girish Karnad has returned to the Hindu epics to create plays dealing with contemporary concerns. The Marae Theatre of New Zealand, established in 1980, has been devoted to enriching drama by use of the traditional performance spaces and religious practices of the Maori peoples.

Religious theatre in the 20th century

In the West, after a century or more of marginalization, religion reappeared as an important part of the theatre experience in the

20th century. This began with the symbolist movement of the 1890s, which challenged the secularism of the realist theatre with a variety of appeals to the non-secular, ranging from a revived interest in traditional religion, especially Catholicism, to a fascination with a wide range of non-traditional occult ceremonials. Strindberg, a leader of the symbolists and an inspiration to the expressionists, created a whole series of dramas, like his *To Damascus Trilogy*, published between 1898 and 1904, which, though idiosyncratic, were unquestionably religious. Another leader of the movement, William Butler Yeats, was profoundly influenced by Noh drama, and brought both the aesthetics and the religious consciousness of that drama into the modern Western drama.

Other major dramatists of the early 20th century who did not embrace symbolist aesthetics still shared their desire to return drama to its religious base. In the case of the mystic French author Paul Claudel this was Catholicism, in that of T. S. Eliot Anglicanism, but each demonstrated that plays with modern settings and characters could also be stirring religious dramas. Much less conventional but equally spiritual theatrical endeavours were carried out by participants in the turn-of-century occult movement, from which symbolism drew much of its inspiration. Aleister Crowley's 1910 *Rites of Eleusis* sought to restore Greek mystic practices to the London stage, while Rudolf Steiner built a theatre-temple, the Goetheanum, in Switzerland in 1910, for the production of modern mystery plays which are still performed there today. Occultism and theatre remained connected thoughout the century, emerging as a major interest in the 1960s with the wide circulation of the visionary writings of Antonin Artaud. Thanks to Artaud, and the Polish director Jerzy Growtowski, who were deeply influenced by Polish Catholic mysticism, a strongly religious and visionary element entered the experimental theatre of the West during the 1960s.

Although the major theatre of the West remained oriented towards the secular, these religious movements in the avant-garde opened the way for a number of clearly religious dramas to appear even in major commercial theatres. Eugene O'Neill, much influenced by symbolism, numbered several such plays among his works. In 1958 the poet Archibald McLeish achieved a major success in New York with *J. B.*, a modern retelling of the Book of Job, and in 1962 Paddy Chayefsky enjoyed a considerable success with *Gideon*, a story from the Book of Judges. Somewhat more surprising was the great success of two rock operas based on the life of Christ, and clearly growing out of the new spiritualism of the 1960s avant-garde: *Godspell* in 1971 and Andrew Lloyd Webber and Tim Rice's *Jesus Christ Superstar* in 1973.

An equally surprising development in religious drama in the late 20th century was an international revival of interest in the presentation of passion plays in conscious imitation of the medieval tradition. The best known of these, as well as the oldest, is the passion play of Oberammergau in Germany, which dates back to 1634 and, defying the ban of 1777, has been performed with only occasional cancellations, since that time, at first annually and now once every ten years. International package tours to Oberammergau were first organized in 1870 and by the end of the century the productions were attracting hundreds of thousands of spectators (Figure 4). By the end of the century, when a new interest in the spiritual side of humanity, pushed aside by scientific positivism, was emerging, productions like those at Oberammergau took on not only an historical but a sociocultural significance. It is striking that one of the first modern enthusiasts for such work was a leading mathematician and Darwinian, Karl Pearson, who in the 1890s became fascinated with contemporary and medieval German passion plays and argued for their importance, not only as a part of the historical process but for the spiritual dimension they could offer to an increasingly materialistic society. Pearson focused upon the German passion plays because in the decades before he wrote, not only Oberammergau, but a number of towns in German Bavaria and the Austrian Tyrol had re-established this medieval form,

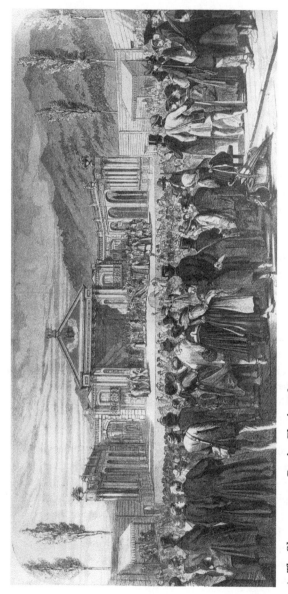

4. The Oberammergau Passion Play in 1860

with growing international attention. By 1930 there were more than 20 such festivals in this region, and leading journals such as the American *Theatre Arts* reported on them as an important part of the world theatre scene.

By that time the concept of the modern passion play was well established outside Europe. The first such production in Mexico was in Iztapalapa, a suburb of Mexico City, which created the work in 1843, like the citizens of Oberammergau two centuries earlier, in thankfulness for delivery from a plague, in this case cholera. On the other side of the globe, in Sri Lanka, the passion plays created at the beginning of the 18th century by Jesuit missionaries and still being performed in several coastal towns were revitalized by the new international interest in such work; one author, Lawrence Perera, even travelled to Oberammergau to gain inspiration for a new Sri Lankan passion play that he introduced in Boralessa in 1923, the first in that country where Jesus was performed by a live actor. In the United States the community spirit which drove the largely patriotic pageant movement at the beginning of the 20th century moved in a number of communities around 1930 into the production of European-style passion plays, and this number increased throughout the century. One of the best known, the Black Hills Passion Play, established in South Dakota in 1932, was created by immigrants from Lünen, Germany, who claimed that they were recreating a performance presented in that city since 1242.

The continuing and complex history of this tradition was suggested by Sarah Ruhl's ambitious 2010 *Passion Play*, with three acts dealing with passion performances in different eras and places: 16th century England, Oberammergau in 1934, and South Dakota in 1984. Britain was not involved in the first wave of such revivals but restagings of cycles in York and Chester were an important part of the British Festival of 1951 and York in particular has since maintained an important modern tradition of such work.

Closely related to the widespread revival of interest in passion plays in the early 1930s was the establishment in 1937 of one of the best-known examples of American pageant theatre, that at Hill Cumorah in upstate New York. The Cumorah Pageant is a religious history drama very similar to the cycle plays of medieval England, beginning with the Creation and including the life of Christ, but then going on to Christ's later ministry in the New World, the revisionist Christian story at the heart of Mormonism. Mormonism is the only major religion developed in the United States and was the most successful of the many religious movements developed in the United States during the early 19th century, in a period of religious fervour known as the Second Great Awakening (the first, a century earlier, brought an evangelical and revival movement into American and British Protestantism). Mormonism dates its founding from the discovery of its sacred text, *The Book of Mormon*, written on golden plates discovered, by angelic direction, by its founder, Joseph Smith. Subsequently driven westward by persecution, the Mormons settled in Utah, which remains their major home, but a century after their founding, in the 1920s, they began to hold ceremonies and stage short plays depicting religious history back in upstate New York, where Joseph Smith found the tablets. Doubtless in part inspired by the widespread American interest in passion plays at this time, a major pageant showing the history of the Church from Biblical times onwards was first presented in 1937 and continues today, one of America's best-known religious pageants.

Somewhat ironically, the most popular production on Broadway as this is written (2013) is a musical, *The Book of Mormon*, a satire on Mormonism and its history, which includes not only references to the Cumorah pageant but a parody of a religious play created by contemporary Mormon missionaries in Africa, very much in the tradition of the Jesuit missionaries in New Spain more than 400 years earlier. Although *The Book of Mormon* is a special case, it suggests the role of religion in the contemporary Western, and especially Anglo-Saxon theatre. Even though traditional passion plays remain popular, often as much for touristic interests as for religious ones, the sort of contemporary religious theatre represented by Eliot and Claudel can be found on major stages today. No new examples of the sort of New Age revivalism represented by *Godspell* or *Jesus Christ Superstar* have appeared either, although both of these are occasionally revived as period pieces. Religion has not disappeared, but appears in revisionist versions, reflecting the disillusionment of a sceptical age, as can be seen in Tony Kushner's 1993 epic *Angels in America*, the most highly acclaimed American drama in recent decades, which draws heavily upon Mormonism and depicts a universe from which God has departed. The more recent *The Testament of Mary* by the Irish writer Colm Tóibin, staged in 2013, depicts Jesus's mother in old age, complaining about the attempts of her son's disciples to turn an ordinary man into a god.

Both *Angels in America* and *The Testament of Mary* reflect the current attitude of the Western drama towards religion, which is not precisely critical, but somewhat nostalgic, looking back on a time when traditional religious faith, which modern scepticism can no longer accept, provided a more comfortable and secure universe. Like all nostalgia, this is hardly an accurate picture, but as the 21st century begins, religion and theatre remain generally separated in the major theatres of the West. Nevertheless, with the global crises engendered by the exceedingly non-religious operations of late capitalism, it is worth recalling the comments of Karl Pearson a century ago, who urged his own society to seek in the spirit of the passion plays a corrective to secular capitalism's cruel indifference to the most vulnerable members of that society.

Chapter 3
Theatre and drama

Like theatre, the word drama has a variety of different meanings in English, but when placed in conjunction with theatre, especially in terms of a field of study, as in a university Department of Theatre and Drama, this combination implies that the department is studying both the written texts (drama) and the performance of them (theatre). As I discussed in my opening chapter, the connection between these two has been extremely close in all eras of the Western theatre, where from the Greeks onward the normal practice has been that someone first creates a written text and subsequently that person and/or others enact that text before audiences. This close connection between theatre and literature is, as I have noted, not found in all theatrical cultures (and for that matter not universal in the West itself). In order to move beyond Western assumptions, then, I will consider in this chapter the source and status of the material being performed on stage, whether it originates as a written text or not.

Improvisation

Although they make up a fairly small part of the world's theatre, there are performances in many cultures that are spontaneously created, the dialogue and action being created on the spot. There is abundant evidence that such improvised entertainments have in many and perhaps most cultures been well developed before anyone set down a text for performance or developed a tradition of repeating the same or similar theatrical actions. Individual court entertainers presenting improvised material, often of a satiric nature, are recorded in China and the Middle East centuries before any written dramatic texts are found.

The dithyrambs, songs honouring the god Dionysius, were, according to Aristotle, the precursors of classical Greek tragedy, and although these became literary compositions as time passed, they began as improvised ecstatic expressions by the poet-actor who led the dithyrambic chorus, speaking the lines inspired as the god entered his body. Less respectable, but far more ubiquitous than the dithyrambic choruses, were improvised ribald skits poking fun at traditional mythological or historical figures as well as common situations in everyday life. Such entertainments are a part of popular culture around the world, but they have been particularly well studied in classical and pre-classical Greece and Rome, in the Megaran farces that predated classical Greek comedy, in the Etruscan revels in pre-classical Rome, and in the better-known Atellan farces and early mimes, all well documented by the 3rd century BCE and doubtless much older than that.

Commedia dell'arte

The theatrical tradition most associated with improvisation is the commedia dell'arte, created in Italy in the mid 16th century, a central part of European theatre for the next two centuries, and still today an influence and a living form especially in Europe but also around the world. Although commedia dell'arte became, by the 18th century, the standard term for work in this tradition, its original title was commedia all'improviso, improvised comedy, stressing its difference from the literary comedy, based on texts, that was being created at that time by pioneering Renaissance dramatists.

This sort of improvised theatre is, however, much less spontaneous than the ecstatic verses of a Dionysian chorus leader or the spontaneous satires of a Chinese court entertainer. The commedia dell'arte was a complex blend of established and free elements. To begin with, the commedia was invariably a group creation, performed by a company of around ten actors, often family members, who normally remained together for years. Each actor performed a specific role with specific relationships to other roles. The origins of the commedia are not known, but there are interesting similarities to the Atellan farces of the Roman Empire, which also had stock figures wearing grotesque masks. A typical commedia company would have two pairs of young lovers, who did not wear masks, and a variety of masked characters, primarily servants and comic men, most commonly the miserly Pantalone, the braggart Spanish captain, and the pedantic doctor. Each of these had a traditional mask and costume and predictable concerns. Although there was no written script, most companies performed form script outlines, called *scenarii*, which provided the general content and characters in each scene. Within that the commedia actors improvised their lines and business, although here also there was a mixture of spontaneous and set material. Every actor had memorized a number of set speeches or physical actions, called *lazzi*, which could be inserted into a scene when thought appropriate.

Although the commedia and derived forms, such as the popular English Punch and Judy puppet shows, the French pantomimed harlequinades, or the German Hanswurst comedies, continued to operate in this essentially improvised form in later centuries, dramatic authors, most notably Molière, by the middle of the 17th century were drawing upon commedia plots and characters to create set literary texts. A century later, Carlo Goldoni, in Venice, a possible birthplace of the form, specifically took it as his mission to give the form literary status by creating scripted texts using commedia subject matter.

Oral traditions

Improvised theatre within the Western tradition from the 18th century onward primarily existed in minor venues, the product of popular street, nightclub, or fairground entertainers, while the theatre became associated almost exclusively with the presentation of the written text, the drama. In the non-Western world, however, especially in areas with a strong tradition of oral performance, popular and community theatre based on improvisation and audience participation remains today the most familiar form of theatre. Africanists of the past century often contrasted Europe and sub-Saharan Africa on the grounds that Europe had progressed from an oral culture to a literary one, while Africa remained predominantly a region of oral culture. With the rise of modern interest in orality, the implied value judgement of this division, with oral culture considered more primitive and less sophisticated, has much diminished, but its basic observation remains valid. Despite the enormous influence of the colonial project, with its ties to European literacy, oral traditions remain strong in most of Africa, and if anything have been reinforced in recent times by a post-colonial reaction to European influence. Oral theatrical performance in Africa, sacred, secular, and combining the two, still thrives today and in many places, among them Nigeria, Senegal, Zambia, South Africa, and Zimbabwe, is a major part of the cultural scene. Not all such performance is improvised in the manner of the community theatre already mentioned. There is also a tradition of performance that is memorized and passed on as intact as possible from one generation to the next, as is traditionally the case with ritual performances. Moreover, there are blends of improvisation and memorized set sequences, somewhat in the manner of the commedia dell'arte, or in the storytelling tradition found in many parts of the world, as for example in the performances of the traditional storyteller, the hakawati, found throughout the Middle East, or the combination puppeteer and narrator of the

Indonesian shadow theatre, the dalang, who both manipulates and provides the voices for dozens of puppets in productions lasting up to nine hours.

Less common are performances in which a kind of storyteller in fact reads (or chants) from a written text, normally providing the voices and often physical descriptions of actions being carried out at the same time by puppets or by mute human actors. The best-known example of the former is found in the Bunraku theatre of Japan, which from its beginnings in the early 17th century has featured a fully visible chanter (*tayu*) presenting the play from a book spread before him, the *yukahon*. In his elegant costume and his dramatic presentation of all the characters, he forms as important a focus of the audience's attention as the puppets themselves. The mimes and pantomimes of classical Greece and Rome were also accompanied by a single or multiple choric voice that presented the libretto. Whether the libretto was ever actually visible, as in the Bunraku, is not known, but an intriguing illustration to one of the first Renaissance editions of Terence, from around 1400, shows what is clearly intended to represent a mime performance, with a singer and book clearly visible on stage much in the manner of the Bunraku chanter. The illustration combines a variety of elements and cannot be taken as an accurate illustration of any particular production. The book-holding chanter, for example, is identified as 'Calliopius', actually an early editor of Terence, but, until the 15th century, thought to have been Terence's favourite actor. The figures performing before him, by their attitudes, costumes, and masks, seem much more likely to come not directly from classical practice, but from the late classical mimes (Figure 5). Whatever its inaccuracies, however, this illustration shows clearly that at the very beginning of the Renaissance there still existed an assumption, surely based upon cultural memory, of late classical performance with masked actors performing with a reader/chanter visibly accompanying them, text in hand.

5. Renaissance hypothetical reconstruction of a classical performance of Terence

Improvisational theatre, rejecting any such pre-existing text, regained an important role in the Western theatre at the beginning of the 20th century, not at first as a performance technique, but as a tool for actor training, utilized by such major figures as Constantin Stanislavsky in Russia and Jacques Copeau in France, and then by their countless imitators and disciples. Among these was the American Viola Spolin, who in the mid 20th century created a variety of improvisational acting exercises she called Theatre Games, which in turn inspired a major tradition of modern improvisational performance, popularized by such companies as Chicago's The Second City, founded in 1959 by Spolin's son Paul Sills. During the 1960s and 1970s many companies with political concerns, such as Augusto Boal's Forum Theatre in Brazil or the San Francisco Mime Troupe, found improvisation an excellent device for relating directly to their audiences and responding rapidly to political events.

Early non-European dramatic texts

Despite the significant non-literary theatrical traditions such as pantomime, commedia, and modern improvisational theatre, the common assumption throughout the Western world, from classical Greece and Rome onward, was that the art of theatre involved the physical enactment on stage of a pre-existing written text. This assumption was also to be seen in a number of Asian traditions, but was distributed to most of the rest of the globe by the colonial project, beginning with the Spanish Conquest in the 15th century and continuing until the spread of independence among the former colonies during the 20th century. With the worldwide dominance of this model, many oral texts that had been performed for generations without any written notation have been converted into written texts by Western authors. Thus the best-known drama of the Incas, the *Apu Ollantay*, which has been claimed to have existed in oral form since the 16th century, did not exist in written form until it was set down in Spanish in the 1780s by Antonio Valdez. Another major surviving drama is the *Rab'inal Achi* of Guatemala, a Mayan dance drama from the 15th century first written down by a French priest in 1856. More recently anthropologists and subsequently theatre scholars have provided written versions of a wide range of oral theatre material from the non-Western world.

Many parts of that world, however, have a long tradition of written drama. Sanskrit was primarily a literary language, mainly used for court records and similar material. The plays created in this language, fragments of which exist from the first century of the Christian era, typically privileged language over action, with lengthy poetic passages and much action placed offstage and revealed by narration. In south-east Asia written epics have existed since the 9th century, and it may be that dramatic texts were created that early, but if so, no trace of them remains. By the 15th century many Indian-influenced palaces and temples possessed a variety of Sanskrit texts, and from this time onward actors are assumed to have drawn on this material. James Brandon, the leading English authority on the theatre of this region, has argued that from this and other sources, theatre managers created 'handbooks' which were used much in the manner of commedia scenarii, providing outlines of plays with bits of dialogue, songs, and other material around which the actors would create a performance, partly by improvisation but primarily with material handed down by oral tradition. Brandon notes the appearance of written dramatic texts in Javanese courts by the end of the 18th century, but considers this an exception to general practice in south-east Asia, which continued to work with written scenarios and dialogue handed down orally. This did not change significantly with a rise in literacy nor the introduction of printing. Even today the *wayang kulit*, Indonesia's most significant dramatic form, is presented without a governing text, although performances have been recorded in written form and subsequently presented as more conventional dramatic texts by Western translators, including Brandon himself.

Plays based upon written texts first became a significant part of Chinese theatre during the Yuan period of the 13th and 14th centuries, but an even greater emphasis on the written text characterized the Japanese Noh developed at almost the same time. Despite the visual spectacle of the Noh drama, it has been from its creation by Zeami solidly based on the written text. The Noh repertoire today consists of about 250 plays, which dictate the costumes, style, and performance details of all sorts. At the heart of this repertoire are the plays of Zeami himself, which make up more than one-third of the repertoire and established the style and structures that later works followed. The subsequent Kabuki and Noh, both derived in large part from the Noh also, despite the major importance of visual spectacle to both, are based upon written texts. This is particularly clear in the Bunraku, where the singer/narrator (*tayu*), in an elaborate traditional costume and with the text open in front of him, delivers that text from the side of the stage, next to the musicians. Like a traditional storyteller, he serves as the narrator and all of the individual characters,

6. **The narrator (*tayu*) in a Bunraku theatre**

varying his voice, gestures, and facial expressions to suggest each character. Thus he shares visual focus with the puppets on stage, the audience watching this presenter of the text as much as they do the onstage action (Figure 6).

Early Western dramatic texts

In the Western tradition, the dramatic text has held a central position for much longer and more consistently than in any other theatre culture. As I have noted earlier, Aristotle privileged the literary side of theatre by dividing poetic creation into epic, lyric, and dramatic and by analysing these basically on literary grounds, virtually ignoring the physical aspect of the drama; this distinction, with its emphasis on the literary text, has remained a common feature of European writings on the theatre ever since. This close connection between the written text and the stage performance of it was reinforced by the close connection between specific texts and specific performances and performance traditions throughout most of Western theatre history. In modern times, the dramatic text and the performance or performances of that text have normally quite separate existences. Even when a play is written for a particular company or (more commonly in the major commercial theatre in the United States) for a particular group of artists specifically assembled to present this play and then dispersed, the published version of this play, if it is published, is then put on the market and freely circulated. Anyone who is willing to pay whatever copyright fees are required may produce the play in other theatres with other production conditions.

Before the 19th century, when dramatic texts began to be more widely circulated, the situation in the West was generally quite different. While written texts were the basis of production, these texts generally remained the property of the theatre or the company for which they were originally created. In Elizabethan England, for example, playwrights would normally sell their plays to a particular theatre company which would then in theory be the only group to present that text. Before the age of publication, often only a single complete copy of this text existed, the company prompt book, to which were added directions for lighting and sound, entrances and exits, all the notes needed to guide the physical presentation of the piece. Despite an underground circulation of pirate texts created by persons who surreptitiously reproduced material from plays they attended as presumed audience members, the connection of any particular text to a particular theatre and group of actors remained strong. With the coming of the age of printing, drama joined the other literary arts in this major new mode of circulation, but not quickly or automatically, since even though dramatists as important as Shakespeare were creating texts that have since been acknowledged as literary masterpieces, there still existed at the time these texts were first written the general feeling that these were only for the use of actors and that there was a considerable gulf between a literary work, which would seek publication, and a theatrical one, which would not.

About half of Shakespeare's plays were in fact published soon after their first presentation, but this did not confer upon them a literary status, since they were published in quartos, the publication size popularly utilized from the invention of printing until this time for all manner of pamphlets, sermons, ballads, and other ephemeral work. A larger printing format, the folio, was used for more expensive and serious literary works, and when Jonson collected his works in a folio, the first English dramatist to do so, it clearly marked a claim for his work to be judged on literary grounds. Jonson's Folio appeared in 1616, the year of Shakespeare's death, and the first Folio collection of Shakespeare's plays did not appear until seven years later.

The regulation of texts

The publication of dramatic texts presented an opportunity for a much wider circulation of these texts theatrically, since alternative venues no longer needed to rely upon the highly unstable pirated versions, but in fact such circulation was severely limited during the 17th and 18th centuries. During those centuries, published versions were intended for reading or in some cases for the use of amateur groups, since the only professional production of most published plays was confined by strict governmental regulation to the particular state-sponsored theatres where these plays were created. As early as 1402, the Confrérie de la Passion was granted a monopoly on the performance of religious plays in Paris, and in 1582, although specifically religious plays were no longer allowed, this company was the single group allowed to perform plays within Paris or its vicinity. Thus the precedent was established from the beginning of the European Renaissance for the Comédie Française and for the many European national theatres established upon the same general model to have their own repertoire of plays, which no other theatre could present. Thus, until the Revolution, only the Comédie was permitted to present the work of Molière, Racine, and the many other dramatists whose work was first presented by that company.

This governmental practice reinforced a far closer and more ongoing relationship between individual dramatic texts and their stage interpretation than has been the case since the rise of Romanticism. The almost universal model of theatre organization in the West, and especially in Europe, has traditionally followed that model found wherever in the world ongoing professional theatres have been established. Such theatres almost invariably have had at their core a group of actors, in some cases related family members, who work together over a long period of time, perhaps for decades. Like other crafts and trades, theatre has often operated through some form of the master–apprentice system, with new members of the company being trained by the older and established members, with the general expectation that they would in turn succeed those mentors and become themselves mentors of the next generation. Their instruction would as a rule not only involve general physical and vocal techniques, but a particular way of performing a particular play, even a particular role or type of role. The Noh theatre is especially well known for its carefully preserved performance tradition, with essentially the same gestures, costumes, and movement accompanying the same words in performance after performance of the same work. Up until the late 18th century, and in some cases through the 19th, most Western theatres also followed a similar if somewhat less strict preservation of particular performance techniques. Not only were young actors trained in certain 'lines of business' as the English called them, or *emplois* according to the French, placing them in such general categories as witty maids, ingénues, or irascible old men, but each type and often even each particular character in a particular play utilized movements, even gestures and line readings that were faithfully passed down, like the movements in Noh, from master to apprentice. When one adds to this lineage of training the fact that a particular play could only be performed by a particular theatre, all organized according to this pattern, a very close connection between a dramatic text and even small details in its interpretation could be seen for much of the early modern theatre in Europe.

Textual dominance

This very close connection between the drama and the stage was most clearly manifested in France, especially from the mid 17th century onward, where the rule-oriented domination of neoclassical thought, the power of tradition, and the detailed regulation of the theatre along with almost every aspect of public life reinforced this connection and discouraged any significant changes in it. Such concerns as Hamlet's, that the clowns 'speak no more than is set down for them', would have been unthinkable on the French neoclassical stage, especially with serious dramas required to strictly follow the rigid demands of the traditional poetic form, the Alexandrine, which gave an individual actor almost no opportunity to change a word, and very little to change the inflection of any line. The dominance of the French theatre on the continent ensured that this power of the text over the production was found from Spain to Russia, where during the 18th century the neoclassical theories and dramas of Voltaire reigned supreme, and dramatists attempted, with varying success, to impose Alexandrine form on such unsuitable languages as Danish.

Despite a flirtation with French practice in the late 17th century, England took a much more liberal view of the relationship between the literary and the performance text, as may be most clearly seen in the works of Shakespeare, who, as he grew steadily in popularity and centrality to the British repertoire, also moved further and further away from the kind of textual fidelity the French continued to give to their classical authors. During the 17th and 18th centuries in England, the gulf between the plays of Shakespeare as they were studied and read as drama and these same works as they were performed in British theatres grew wide indeed. Producers freely added, omitted, or rearranged lines, scenes, and characters. Tragedies like *King Lear* and *Romeo and Juliet* were restructured with happy endings. Music and spectacle were added to plays like *Macbeth*. David Garrick, the greatest British theatre figure of his time and an ardent devotee of Shakespeare, claimed in the late 18th century to reject this practice and to return Shakespeare's own words to the stage, but although his championship of this project doubtless encouraged other later producers, there still remained a great difference between any Garrick production and anything like an accurate Shakespearian text.

Garrick's vision of placing Shakespeare's exact words on stage became a major project during the 19th century, when a growing cultural interest in historical research in general led to a careful study of the Quartos and Folios, the ongoing attempt to assemble a definitive text from them and a concern on the part of many theatre organizations to present productions faithful to the original text. The written drama and the performed play grew closer together than they had been since the English Renaissance. Closely related to this was an historicist interest in England and elsewhere in presenting the plays not only in their original words, but in something like their original performance conditions. The Romantic dramatist Ludwig Tieck introduced this concern to the German theatre early in the 19th century, and it was most fully realized near the end of the century in the influential productions of William Poel and his Elizabethan Stage Society, which between 1895 and 1911 presented a series of dramas by Shakespeare and his contemporaries on a stage attempting to recreate the performance conditions of Shakespeare's era.

This interest in modern historicism grew out of the Romantic movement, which internationally looked to Shakespeare as its central inspiration, but Romantic thought by no means encouraged in general the converging of drama and theatre. On the contrary, some of the leaders of this movement, among them Charles Lamb in England and Goethe in Germany, viewed the staging of Shakespeare with great suspicion and argued that his full genius could be experienced only by approaching his work as literary drama and not as scripts for stage presentation. Their concern was that Shakespeare, as a Romantic genius, had expressed his vision directly through his words and that anything added by physical performance, however effective, would dilute, diminish, or distract from the purity of the original expression. The concern that any stage interpretation limits or distorts the purity of the artist's original vision is still expressed by some critics with a literary orientation today, and continues to provide tension between champions of the printed and the performed text.

Challenges to the text

Nor were such concerns expressed only by literary theorists. At almost the same time that both literary and theatrical scholars were attempting to discover and to stage a text as close as possible to Shakespeare's original words, a movement was developing among theatre theorists that worked in almost direct opposition to this, driving a wedge between theatre and the literary drama. Probably the most influential leader of this movement was the English theorist and designer Edward Gordon Craig, who insisted that theatre break free from its reliance upon literature and develop into a distinct art form based not upon words, but upon rhythm, sound, light, and moving forms. Instead of looking to the playwright as the controlling agent of the production, Craig championed an emerging theatre artist, the modern director, who would be the one primarily responsible for the total effect of the theatrical production.

The question of whether the literary text (and its production tradition) or the vision of the director should be ultimately the defining element in the production has been a continuing and often passionate source of controversy ever since the coming to prominence of the director at the end of the 19th century. During the latter part of the century, when in many parts of the globe major directors such as Peter Brook, Giorgio Strehler, or Ariane Mnouchkine became better known than any contemporary dramatists from their countries, this controversy increased. Continental European directors often so dominated the dramatic texts they were utilizing that the German term *Regietheater* (director's theatre) gained wide prominence, sometimes as a neutral descriptive term, but often as a term of opprobrium. Although this sort of controlling director was particularly associated with continental Europe, similar figures appeared around the globe; Yokio Ninagawa or Tadashi Suzuki from Japan, Victor Garcia from Argentina, or Ong Keng Sen from Singapore are a few examples among many.

If many theatre practitioners from Gordon Craig onward have encouraged a separation of the drama and the theatre, particularly by elevating the director over the playwright as the controlling artist in the production, theatre scholars also added to this separation in a different way, by developing theatre studies as a new discipline, distinct from literature. It is surely not coincidental that these parallel movements in theatre practice and theatre studies began to be articulated at almost the same time, in the closing years of the 19th century and the opening years of the 20th.

Drama and theatre in the university

Literature was developed as a university discipline during the 18th century, and the study of drama in the various national languages was considered essentially as a subdivision of literature. The physical conditions of performance were essentially ignored, as having no more to do with the study of drama, in the words of Joel Spingarn, a leading literary theorist of early 20th century America, than a history of printing had to do with the study of poetry. The first scholars of theatre, who appeared at the turn of the 20th century, came from literature departments, took exception to this view, and thus aroused no small opposition from their former colleagues. Brander Matthews was named by Columbia University in 1900 as the first Professor of Dramatic Literature in an English-speaking university and although this title would not necessarily suggest it, he took as his mandate the study of theatre in performance. This distinction was clearer in the case of the first European scholar to make a similar break, Max Herrmann in Germany, who gave his first lectures on theatre in 1900 and in 1923 in Berlin left the established field of *Literaturewissenschaft* (literature studies) to found, despite much opposition from colleagues, the first institute for *Theaterwissenschaft* (theatre studies). Since these pioneering efforts, theatre has been generally accepted as an academic field of study in most Western universities, but despite the common title of this field as 'Theatre and Drama' in the United States, there still remains tension in many schools over whether artists like Shakespeare should properly be taught in theatre or literature departments.

The exact relationship between theatre and drama was one of the central concerns of the most influential critical approach to these subjects (and to many others) in the mid 20th century, semiotics. At first developed by a group of cultural and linguistic theorists in Prague during the 1930s and 1940s, semiotic theory re-emerged as a major tool for the analysis of all manner of cultural phenomena in the 1960s and impacted theoretical discourse around the world. A central concern of semiotic analysis as it was applied to theatre in fact dealt with the question of analysing the exact working relationship between the written drama and its performance in the theatre. Semiotic theorists, whose strategies were originally derived from linguistic analysis, generally sought to see the products of human culture as 'texts' to be analysed in terms of their ability to communicate messages. Thus they often spoke of the drama as the 'written text' and its realization in the theatre as the 'performative text'. Anne Ubserfeld, a leading French theatre semiotician, suggested that the written text was incomplete, consciously left with gaps (she called it 'troué', having 'holes') to be filled in by theatrical realization. This view was not widely accepted by many theatre semioticians who, with a more literary bias, were much more comfortable with the traditional view of the written drama as an artistic creation complete in its own right, whether it was ever realized in the theatre or not. The general view among such scholars was to treat these two texts essentially as different languages, so that the process of staging a play involved translating a written text into a performative one, which, like any translation, sought to find close equivalents but recognized that the translation inevitably made significant changes not only to the form of the underlying 'message' but inevitably to its content as well.

In the late 20th century, a new dimension was added to this long-standing negotiation in the Western world between the literary drama and the performed play by the rise of performance studies. I have already discussed many of the implications of this new approach to theatre in my chapter on this subject, but I will only note here that performance, with its orientation toward the process of enactment, has largely reinforced the already existing gulf between the written drama and its staging. The growing international influence of this new orientation has ensured that the focus of performance studies upon enactment and the corresponding weakening of the bonds between such enactment and a pre-existing literary text has strengthened this separation in many parts of the globe.

Postdramatic theatre

One of the most widely quoted recent theoretical statements on theatre has been Hans-Thies Lehmann's 1999 *Postdramatic Theatre*. Although Lehmann focuses his study on the Western theatrical theory and practice from around the 1970s onward, he looks back to the avant-gardes of the early 20th century, the championing of the director as an independent artist by Craig and others, and particularly to Peter Szondi's *Theory of the Modern Drama*, published in German in 1956 and translated into English in 1987. Such unfortunate delay in the translation into English of major texts in other languages is less today, but still surprising. While Szondi's work waited 30 years for such a translation, Lehmann's waited only seven, until 2006. Even so, the English translation was preceded by translations into French and Japanese in 2002, into Slovenian and Croatian in 2003, into Polish in 2004, and into Farsi in 2005. The fact that this book was accessible in Japan and Iran years before it appeared in English translation not only indicates the conservatism of English-language scholarship concerning that produced in other languages, but, more importantly, suggests how much theatrical theory, like theatrical practice, is involved today in a process of global circulation.

In the prologue to his book, Lehmann argues that for centuries the European theatre has been dominated by a paradigm that sharply distinguishes it from the theatres of other parts of the world such as the dance dramas of India or the Noh of Japan. While these latter forms are dominated by dance, music, highly stylized and choreographed movements, spectacular costumes, and other visual elements, the European drama has been primarily concerned with the stage enactment of dramatic texts. Even when music, dance, or spectacle was added or even became dominant elements, the written text remained the central determining part of the event.

The human figure, as in almost all world theatre, remained the core element of the production, but that figure was primarily characterized not through any physical or vocal display but through speech, and that speech was in turn determined by and founded upon the pre-existing dramatic text.

Lehmann sees his project as in certain respects an extension of that of Szondi, who in mid century felt that the central characteristic of the modern theatre was that it was becoming more and more separated from the drama. Szondi, looking to the experiments of Brecht, Pirandello, and the expressionists, saw them all as attempts to break away from the stability of the text-based drama and its conventions of dialectic discourse, evolving narrative, character depiction, and mimesis. Looking particularly to Brecht, he proposed rejecting the term dramatic in favour of epic for a more open form more compatible with a rapidly changing view of the world and of the human subject.

Lehmann, looking to the experimental work of artists like Robert Wilson, Tadeusz Kantor, or Tadashi Suzuki, notes the tendency of such work to depart, as neither the conventional dramatic theatre nor Brecht's epic theatre does, from a dramatic action/plot, a composed course of action largely based upon the conventions of mimesis and the fictive world. The work of these and other recent experimental theatre artists has moved from narration to event, from a text-based story told to passive spectators to an action which may well involve the active participation of its viewers, from a theatre that calls for understanding and comprehension to one that is based upon experience and open-ended association. To such a theatre Lehmann gives the name postdramatic, a term which, since the appearance of his book, has gained wide international circulation.

This is not, of course, to say that the break of the long-held bond between theatre and drama especially in the West is in the process of dissolving. Most theatregoers and most critics still consider this the basis of the theatrical experience, and with the global reach of Western practice the 'modern drama' internationally still generally assumes this bond. Nevertheless, the continuing challenge to a theatre separated from drama, which has been at the heart of Western experimental performance now for more than a century, has come to be accepted as a significant part of this art, and so for the foreseeable future theatre seems sure to be involved with both dramatic and postdramatic manifestations.

Chapter 4
Theatre and performance

During the last quarter of the 20th century, the term performance gained an ever-greater prominence in relation to theatre studies, first in the United States, then in Europe, and by the end of the century, around the world, owing in significant measure to the predominant position that Europe, especially Western Europe, and the United States held in theatre studies and in the development and the dissemination of new theories and practices in this and related fields. As performance became increasingly a matter of concern to theatre scholars in Europe and the United States, its spread to other parts of the globe was inevitable.

Although some variation of the word theatre can be found in many European languages, doubtless due to the general European agreement that this art originated in classical Greece, from which the term is drawn, the linguistic background of the term performance is quite different. Like many modern English words, the ancestry of 'perform' is French, from the Old French term 'parfournir' meaning 'to do' or 'to carry out'. Although the modern French word 'fourni' (and the closely related English word 'furnish') is descended from 'parfournir', there is no modern French word corresponding to performance, especially in the many rather varied meanings it has developed in English. The same is true of the other Romance languages, and of other European languages as well. Thus, although the term performance is now familiar around the world, it is as a borrowed modern English term, like 'computer' or 'Internet'. Along with the term have been borrowed various applications of the term, almost entirely derived ultimately from theorists in the United States, where the modern concept of performance developed. Even there, the term refers to a wide range of phenomena, but the best way to gain an idea of the implications of performance, and its impact on theatre, is to begin with its development and the concerns it has addressed in the United States. There the modern usage of the term developed along with various models of its relationship to theatre.

Performance and the art world

The modern interest in performance can be traced to several different developments in the early 1970s, in the art world, in academic theatre, and in the social sciences, particularly sociology and anthropology. Within the art world, a certain interest in the operations of the live body as an artistic medium, quite distinct from the concerns of traditional theatre, can be found in various experimental art movements throughout the 20th century, in futurism, in Dada, in the happenings of Allan Kaprow, in the work of Fluxus, but on the whole these remained confined to the world of the visual arts. Indeed, some of the most influential artists involved with such work, such as Kaprow, specifically denied any association with theatre, with its already fixed procedures, assumptions, and rules.

In the early 1970s, works particularly concerned with the activities of the living body became an increasingly important part of the conceptual art movement outside the boundaries of traditional artistic materials. The terms 'body art', 'performance art', and sometimes 'life art' then began to be applied to such work. Some of these followed the example of the Kaprow happenings of the previous decades, displaying everyday activities such as walking, sleeping, eating, or drinking. Others pushed the body to extreme

7. Chris Burden, *Shoot*, 1971. Burden's statement: 'At 7:45 p.m. I was shot in the left arm by a friend. The bullet was a copper jacket .22 long rifle. My friend was standing about fifteen feet from me.'

physical conditions, even to real danger, most notoriously perhaps in the 1971 performance piece *Shoot*, in which a friend of the artist Chris Burden shot him in the arm with a real rifle bullet (Figure 7).

While such spectacular examples of performance attracted the most attention from the media, these extreme cases represented only a very small part of what was becoming a very important new means of artistic expression, located somewhere between theatre and conceptual art and involving the living body, usually appearing alone. Although Kaprow and others continued to demand a separation of performance art from theatre, the two forms grew steadily closer together during the 1970s. Perhaps most important in this convergence was feminist performance, which almost by definition was rarely if ever totally devoid of discursive content and which often followed a long tradition of monologue performance in the theatre but devoted to the specific topic of the experience, often autobiographical, of women in contemporary society. Men and male performance dominated early performance art but the 1970s saw a flourishing of feminist performance, reflecting the rapid growth during that decade of women's concerns throughout art and culture, especially in the United States. Southern California took an early lead in such work, with artists like Linda Montano and Rachel Rosenthal, but New York was another important centre, with many of the best-known women performance artists, including Yoko Ono, Carolee Schneeman, and Laurie Anderson.

The term 'performance' in the English theatre tradition

While the concept and practice of performance art were growing in importance and visibility (by the 1980s the *New York Times* Arts and Leisure section regularly included a division 'performance' alongside 'theatre' and 'music'), the term 'performance' was during these same years taking on a new significance in the social sciences and in the theatre. The term performance has had a long association with theatre in the English language, though not, as has been noted, in other, even closely related European languages. The verb 'perform' goes back to the late Middle Ages, but by the time of Shakespeare, it had developed a particular association with the presentation of theatrical and musical works. The noun 'performance' is said to have been first used in 1709 by Richard Steele in an early issue of his journal *The Tatler*, in reference to a benefit presented by the actor Thomas Betterton. Since that time, a performance has become the common English term to indicate either the work of an actor on a particular theatrical occasion, as in 'Richard Burton's performance of Hamlet was outstanding,' or to refer to the theatrical occasion itself, as in 'The play ran for 300 performances.' It is, in English, a term as familiar as 'theatre' or 'drama'. During the 1970s, however, the term 'performance' began to be used with distinctly different connotations, so much separating itself from theatre that today academic departments, conferences, and publications devoted to 'theatre *and* performance' can be found throughout the English-speaking world, and indeed beyond. Although this shift occurred within the world of academic theatre studies, it was essentially inspired by developments in other academic disciplines, particularly the social sciences, not by the appearance and proliferation during this same decade of modern performance art, which would seem a more direct possible influence.

The 'performative turn' in the social sciences

A major shift in methodological orientation took place in the social sciences in the 1950s to 1970s, which has come to be known as the 'performative turn'. A major figure in this shift was Kenneth Burke, an American literary theorist and philosopher, who was one of the first to employ theatrical language and metaphors to aid in the understanding of social and cultural phenomena, an approach he referred to as 'dramatism'. In his two key books, *A Grammar of Motives* and *A Rhetoric of Motives*, he analysed human interaction as a series of events more or less consciously 'staged' to produce certain effects upon others. This approach, turning away from more abstract symbolic and structural models to study everyday interactions and the communicative strategies of embodied practice, characterized much of the most important and innovative work during the following decades in anthropology, sociology, ethnography, psychology, and linguistics.

Once introduced, the concept of performance as an analytical tool spread rapidly across the social sciences; indeed, one can trace its emergence to a few years at the end of the 1950s. A central figure in this process was the sociologist Erving Goffman, arguably the most influential American sociologist of the 20th century. In his most influential work, the 1959 *The Presentation of Self in Everyday Life*, Goffman developed in some detail the approach he called, in conscious or unconscious echoing of Burke, 'dramaturgical analysis'. The opening chapter of this book was entitled 'Performance', which Goffman defined as 'all the activity of an individual which occurs during a period marked by his continual presence before a particular set of observers and which has some influence on the observers'. Although Goffman applied this definition to a wide variety of social interactions, one can see how close it comes to a theatrical model by realizing that it could, with equal accuracy, be used to describe almost all of the performance art of the coming decades and for that matter any traditional solo theatrical presentation.

In anthropology the British scholar Victor Turner, whose reputation within his own field rivalled that of Goffman in sociology, played a similar role introducing a performative orientation. This was first clearly articulated in Turner's 1957 work *Schism and Continuity*. Although its subject matter, a study of the Ndembu tribe of Zambia, was quite conventional, the approach was structured in dramaturgical forms. In studying the dynamics by which societies moved from one mode of organization to another, Turner coined the term 'social drama', turning, like Burke, to a kind of predictable dramatic structure in this process.

Turner's orientation was reinforced by the American anthropologist Milton Singer, who introduced the now widely used term 'cultural performance' in a collection of essays on Indian culture that he edited in 1959. Singer urged the study of such performance as providing the most concrete observable units of the structure of a culture. Although he focuses on the group and not the individual, his definition of a cultural performance is strikingly similar to Goffman's definition of a performance, and again, although this is not Singer's focus, would serve perfectly well to describe a traditional theatre event. The defining features of a cultural performance, according to Singer, were a specifically limited timespan, a clear beginning and end, an organized programme of activity within this span, a set of performers, an audience, and a specific place and occasion.

Speech–act theory

The third major contribution to modern performance theory came from the field of linguistics, and especially in the development of speech–act theory. The foundations of this approach were laid in in a lecture series delivered at Harvard by John Austin in 1955 which was published under the title *How to Do Things with Words*. Here Austin called attention to a particular use of language, which he called 'performative'. In such speech, the words do not merely assert something, as in most language, but also actually do something in the real world. His best-known example is the taking of the marriage vows and the minister's pronouncing of the new union. Noam Chomsky, the most influential modern linguistic theorist, also gave new prominence to the term 'performance' in his 1965 *Aspects of the Theory of Syntax*, although his use of the term was different from and more inclusive than Austin's. Here he distinguished between 'competence', a speaker's general knowledge of a language, and 'performance', the specific application of this knowledge in a speech situation.

John R. Searle, a student of Austin's, developed the theory of speech as action further, most notably in his 1969 book *Speech Acts*. Here, instead of designating, as Austin did, only a few special instances of speech as performative, Searle argued that all speech has a performative aspect, in that it expresses the intent of the speaker to have a certain effect on the hearer. A theory of language, he said, was actually part of a theory of action. Thus by the end of the 1960s leading figures in linguistics (Austin and Searle), anthropology (Singer and Turner), and sociology (Goffman) were all proposing the concept of performance as a productive new way to organize and understand the social and cultural material that each of their disciplines were committed to study. Richard M. Dorson, in a 1972 survey article covering the field of folklore studies, which had undergone a similar reorientation during the previous decade, designated the new approach as more 'contextual' and characterized it as involving a shift from a study of the folkloric text to the function of that text as a 'performative and communicative act' in a particular cultural situation.

Although all of these theorists, like Burke before them, drew inspiration for this new approach from the vocabulary of drama and the theatre, few of them gave much attention to theatre as a possible site of application of their developing ideas. Indeed, Austin specifically excluded theatrical speech from his study, on the grounds that performative utterances were in a peculiar way 'hollow or void' when they were pronounced by actors in a theatrical performance. In those circumstances, he asserted, language was not used 'seriously', but in a way he called 'parasitic' upon its normal use. Such misgivings about the operations of theatre were not expressed in France, where at least within the field of sociology a significant disciplinary interest arose in the operations of theatre developed in the mid 1950s, just as the 'performative turn' was beginning to be explored by Anglo-Saxon theorists. This new orientation was introduced by one of the leading sociologists of the period, Georges Gurvitch. Although Gurvitch's major concern was the sociology of knowledge, and in particular of the law, he was instrumental in organizing a pioneering conference in the application of sociological analysis to the theatre, held at Royaumont in France in 1955. He summarized the proceedings of this conference in a remarkably prescient essay 'Sociologie du théâtre', which appeared in 1956. Like Goffman, he called attention to the theatrical element in all social ceremonies, even in simple receptions or a small gathering of friends, and that every individual in the course of his interaction with others plays a variety of 'social roles'. But unlike Goffman, Gurvitch also subjected the theatre itself to sociological analysis, considering how its performers and public were also engaged in performing 'a social action'.

Gurvitch's comments on the 'theatricality' of social life were expanded by other French sociologists and anthropologists during the following years, but his particular attention to theatre was neglected, as these scholars applied a theatrical analysis to the more traditional objects of study in their fields. A good example of such work was Michel Leiris's *La Possession et ses aspects théâtraux chez les Ethiopiens de Gondar*. No scholar took up his challenge to apply such analysis to theatre until 1963, when Jean Duvignaud published his pioneering *Sociologie*, the first major book in any language devoted to this subject. During the 1960s Duvignaud and others continued to develop this field in France, but their work went unnoticed by almost all theatre theorists in England and the United States. The first significant English-language acknowledgement of his work appeared in 1972 in the book *Theatricality* by Elizabeth Burns. In it, Burns argues for a sociological approach to theatre, which, she complains, has up to that time remained 'wholly the concern of French scholars', especially Gurvitch and Duvignaud.

Certainly Burns was correct in noting the provincialism of English-speaking theatre scholars who for almost two decades had remained unaware of this significant new approach to theatre analysis developing in France, though it is somewhat surprising to see that she was unfamiliar with the work of Raymond Williams, who was by this time a prominent figure in the British intellectual world and who more than a decade before had undertaken just this sort of analysis of the drama in his well-known book, *The Long Revolution*. In the opening paragraph of a chapter in this work entitled 'The Social History of Dramatic Forms', Williams began by noting that the nature of the organization of experience in the theatre was in terms of 'performance', and went on to argue that since drama normally operates in a social context, its social history was in many respects easier to analyse than the social history of most of the other arts. By way of illustration, he then proceeded to apply social analysis to a history of the English drama from the medieval period to his own times.

Richard Schechner and *TDR*

Burns also, as an English scholar, was clearly unaware that in the United States an interest in such work (also apparently quite unaware of the French or for that matter of Williams) was clearly developing during these same years. At the centre of this interest was Richard Schechner, who in 1962 had become editor of the *Tulane Drama Review* (renamed *The Drama Review* or simply *TDR* in 1967). During the 1960s Schechner made this journal the most important English-language theatre publication concerned with the various new movements and approaches of that turbulent decade. The journal had begun focusing on dramatic literature, especially new work from Europe such as Genet and Ionesco, but in 1964 Schechner began to focus more on production, featuring The Living Theatre, Stanislavky, and Grotowski. Then, in the summer issue of 1966, Schechner published an essay that would prove the foundational statement of the subsequent performance studies movement in this journal, then in the United States and ultimately internationally.

This essay, 'Approaches to Theory/Criticism', is, significantly, grounded not in traditional theatre scholarship, but in the social sciences, particularly in the work of the Cambridge anthropologists who, in the early 20th century, had a profound influence on speculations about the origins of Greek tragedy. Admitting that these speculations have been largely discredited, Schechner argues that it is time to consider theatre from another dimension, that of its operations as one of the many types of human public performance, along with rituals, play, games, and sports. In a footnote to this key assertion, Schechner quotes Goffman as extending performance potentially to *any* human activity, but states that his concept is much more limited, restricted to an activity undertaken by an individual or a group

Theatre and performance

with the primary goal of bringing pleasure to another individual or group. Attempting to apply the concept of performance to games and sports led Schechner to the major cultural theorists who had analysed the dynamics of play, Johan Huizinga and Roger Caillois, as well as to the more recent work of the Canadian psychiatrist Eric Berne, whose most recent work, *Games People Play*, was cited by Schechner in support of his joining together of ritual, play, and performance.

Eric Berne was briefly an important source for Schechner in this new pursuit. The Summer 1967 issue of the *Tulane Drama Review* featured an article about applying Berne's methodology of transactional analysis to directing, and an interview with Berne entitled 'Notes on Games and Theatre', in which Berne suggested the work of an actor should be considered not as playing a character but as dealing with a series of specific interpersonal transactions.

Schechner did not pursue this interest during the remaining two years of his term as editor, but he significantly returned to it in 1973, when his editorial successor, Michael Kirby, was presenting a series of special issues on such subjects as black theatre, visual performance, and popular entertainments, and asked Schechner to return as guest editor to organize an issue on theatre and the social sciences.

Schechner's lead article, though brief (one and a half pages), takes up the interests he expressed in 1967 and offers a more programmatic view of seven key areas where he argues that performance theory and the social sciences coincide. Schechner was apparently unaware of the similar project by Gurvitch two decades before, but the areas he lists are very similar, including performance in everyday life, including gatherings of all kinds, sports, ritual play, and certain aspects of ethnography and psychotherapy. He mentions Goffman, Levy-Strauss, and Gregory Bateson as important figures not represented in this issue, which

he admits leans heavily on two potential areas out of many—
kinesics and therapy. Indeed, even these are not extensively
represented, with two articles on kinesis and one on occupation
therapy. Schechner concludes this introduction admitting that this
special issue is only a beginning and calling for the establishment
of a journal exclusively devoted to performance theory in which
he promises to collaborate in any way he can.

Such a journal not appearing, Schechner began, very successfully,
to build up a collection of writings on performance theory that
were central in establishing the field. The first gathering of these
appeared in 1976. This was *Ritual, Play, and Performance*, a
collection co-edited by Schechner that fulfilled much more clearly
the goals he had stated in the *TDR* special issue three years before.
In addition to essays by Schechner himself, this book included
work by Levi-Strauss, Huizinga, Bateson, Konrad Lorenz, Jane
Lawick-Goodall, Goffmann, whose work had inspired Schechner
from the beginning, and Victor Turner, who would become
the social scientist most closely associated with Schechner's
development of performance studies. A second collection, *Essays
on Performance Theory 1970–1976*, consisted only of Schechner's
own essays, but others, particularly Goffman and Turner, were
often cited in these.

Turner and Schechner met in 1977 and from then until Turner's
death in 1983 worked closely together. One of the first fruits of
this, two years after their meeting, was the first 'performance
theory' course ever offered at New York University or indeed
in any academic institution. It was headed by Schechner and
Turner but with a visiting faculty of dance scholars,
anthropologists, psychonalysts, semioticians, and experimental
theatre artists. Within a few years, a body of related courses had
developed, the department changed its name to the Department
of Performance Studies, the first in the world, and as early as
1981 a student-edited performance studies newsletter began
to be issued on a regular basis. Its first editor was Jill Dolan,

later to become one of the pioneers in the development of feminist theatre theory.

Schechner returned to editorship of *The Drama Review* in 1986, announcing that the central concern of the journal would become 'performance in all its dimensions', including dance, music, theatre, performance art, popular entertainments, media, movies, sports, rituals, performance in daily life, politics, folk performance, and play. Two years later the journal emphasized this reorientation, as the NYU Drama department had done at the beginning of the decade, by changing its name. No longer *The Drama Review*, it now officially changed to *TDR*, with the subtitle *The Drama Review: A Journal of Performance Studies*. The editors explained that they wished to separate themselves from drama entirely, but were prevented by the protests of library subscribers. Three years later, '*A Journal of Performance Studies*' was adjusted to the less modest, but essentially accurate '*The Journal of Performance Studies*'.

The spread of performance studies

By the mid 1980s, however, New York University no longer was the only institution with a programme in performance studies, nor even the only such programme in the United States. In 1984 the Department of Interpretation at Northwestern University in Chicago changed its name to the Department of Performance Studies, and the following year the first Programme in Performance Studies was established outside the United States, at Aberystwyth University in Wales. During the next decade this new academic discipline appeared in universities around the world, in Europe, India, and as far as Australia. By 1997 its international scope was sufficient to justify the founding of a global organization, Performance Studies International. The United States remains the major location of departments of performance studies, and the field there has been dominated by the two pioneer programmes, at NYU and Northwestern.

Their histories were different and so, in certain measure, have been their emphases and influence.

NYU performance studies, as we have seen, developed out of the theatre programme, and the growing interest of Schechner in the social sciences, and especially in the work of Goffman and Turner. The programme at Northwestern grew instead out of the study of speech and oral communication. It turned toward an interest in performance in its own version of the 'performative turn' involving so many disciplines in the late 20th century, and generally involved in some way with a shift from an emphasis on text to expressive behaviour in general and particularly as such behaviour was then being explored in the social sciences by scholars like Singer, Goffman, and Turner. The central figure in this shift at Northwestern was Dwight Conquergood, an anthropologist, who sought to understand local cultures, both in Chicago and elsewhere in the world, by an analysis of their performance practices.

Although the students and the theoretical statements coming from both of these founding programmes have been central to the development of this field both in the United States and subsequently around the globe, the NYU model has remained more influential in the theatre, so that in addition to specifically performance studies programmes, there are now even more academic programmes that designate themselves by some combination of these terms, such as 'Theatre and Performance Studies' (Stanford, Brown, Maryland, and others). Such blends are widely found in the social sciences, but have rarely been acknowledged as a official academic area (as for example, the School of Theatre, Performance and Cultural Policy Studies at Warwick University in England).

This closer connection of theatre studies with the NYU school is quite understandable since that programme grew out of theatre and was largely driven in its early years by Schechner, a theatre actor and theorist. However, this genealogy also had an unfortunate side effect, which was that Schechner and others correctly or incorrectly felt it necessary as performance studies were being established, to stress the field's independence from theatre, often rather stridently. Probably the key moment in this division was Schechner's keynote address in 1992 to the annual convention of the Association for Theater in Higher Education, the leading academic theatre organization in the United States. The talk was subsequently published as a *TDR* editorial. One central statement from this talk became famous, or notorious: 'The fact is that theatre as we have known and practiced it—the staging of written dramas—will be the string quartet of the 21st century: a beloved but extremely limited genre, a subdivision of performance.' Such statements confirmed traditional theatre scholars, many already suspicious of this new area of study, in their belief that performance studies posed a kind of threat to theatre, arrogantly dismissing it or seeking to absorb it. During the next decade or so a clear tension existed in the United States and to some extent in England between the two approaches, but today, another decade later, this tension has largely disappeared, and theatre and performance have in large part developed a close, even symbiotic, relationship, indicated by the many academic programmes that now include both terms in their titles.

Theatre and performance studies

Under these circumstances it becomes important to ask how theatre has changed as a result of the challenge of and gradual accommodation to performance and performance studies. What have been the results, in the United States and elsewhere, of the association of the long-established term theatre becoming increasingly connected in the 21st century with the newly established term performance? The change has been a profound one, challenging many of the most basic previous assumptions of theatre scholars and practitioners, particularly in the so-called 'West', essentially composed of Europe and the United States, where the modern field of theatre studies was created and developed and where the vast majority of studies of this subject (including, of course, the present one) continue to be produced.

Looking back over a half century of rapidly changing ideas, around the world, about what sort of an activity theatre is and what role it is playing and has played in human culture, it is clear that the rise of performance studies provided theatre studies, as it existed in the middle of the last century, with a variety of fresh perspectives on these questions, at a time when old Eurocentric models of theatre were seen to be increasingly inadequate as knowledge of and interest in theatre-like activities in other cultures in other parts of the world were rapidly expanding. One of the most influential books of the 1960s was Thomas Kuhn's *The Structure of Scientific Revolutions*, which argued that scientific fields did not progress in a linear and consistent manner, but followed a particular set of assumptions that proved over time increasingly unable to accommodate new data. Eventually the strain on the old system became so great that, in what Kuhn famously called a 'paradigm shift', new strategies of understanding and analysis emerged that could better cope with this new material. Kuhn's concept doubtless owed much of its rapid spread to the fact that, for a variety of reasons, many areas of knowledge were at the time undergoing or about to undergo just this sort of major reorientation.

Among these areas was the understanding of theatre, which at that time still followed the long-standing tradition of regarding this art not only as based on literary texts, but on a particular, well-established collection of texts by authors from a very limited group of countries. The 1960s also saw a serious questioning of this exclusivity, in the form of attacks on what was called the 'canon'. When theatre emerged as an independent field of study in the West, at the end of the 19th century, it notably did not challenge the canon already long established by students of literature. Theatre continued to privilege the same, almost entirely

Western European dramatists—Shakespeare, Schiller. Molière, Ibsen—along with a few additional figures from the United States and Russia (O'Neill, Miller, Chekhov), while ignoring almost entirely all of the rest of the world with the very modest token exceptions of the classical Sanskrit drama in India and Japanese Bunraku and Noh. In splitting from scholars of literature, the new theatre scholars shifted their orientation from the study of the images, themes, characters, and structure of these dramatists to a study of their conditions of performance: how they were acted, how they were staged, in what sort of physical space they were presented. The actual works considered to make up the 'theatre', however, did not change—a modest number of mostly Western European male authors of acknowledged literary merit.

In the late 20th century, however, scholars of theatre, like their colleagues in literary studies in different European languages, began to add to their studies of the works in this received canon the dynamics and processes by which this canon had come into being and through which it was maintained. Gradually an awareness grew that the canon, far from being the result of objective and unchanging standards of abstract artistic excellence, had been constructed, sometimes consciously but more often not, in order to demonstrate the supremacy of certain groups—a class, an ethnicity, a nation, a gender—in a self-created and self-justifying system. The first significant challenge to the canonical system, especially in the theatre, came from feminist scholars, but their attack was soon followed by a realization of the inadequacy of the canonical model for a theatre that in the late 20th century sought to redefine itself as a global area of study and production, not simply the Europe-based phenomenon it had been up until that time.

Here again the long-accepted canonical model presented a serious problem, since it contained very few examples of the immense body of non-Western theatre which a new, more global consciousness revealed. The old European high art model provided no way of discussing almost any of this material except as inferior or more primitive forms of what the West had more fully and artistically developed, or as a colourful and exotic cultural activity of interest more to anthropologists and folklorists than to students of theatre. In large measure this was due to the West's historical privileging of the literary text (this phenomenon is discussed in more detail in the section on drama and the theatre) and also the individual performance of that text (particularly the original one) as the primary artistic object of study. This necessarily distorted or precluded serious interest in the many non-Western traditions that did possess such texts or such historical orientations.

Nor were the limitations of this model confined to theatre traditions and individual manifestations outside the European sphere. The study of so-called Western theatre itself was also seriously limited. Even when considering plays safely within the canon, such important theatrical manifestations as the fluidity of texts from performance to performance and even more from revival to revival were largely ignored by a tradition that insisted upon considering a play as if it operated in the same way as an established literary text, moving unchanged through time like a painting or a piece of sculpture. The role of the audience and the social context of each particular production were as a consequence also ignored. Further, of course, popular theatre or any kinds of works that fell outside the canon, even within the European tradition, were given little or no attention except in the rare cases when they could be considered as 'sources' for more respectable literary drama, as the commedia dell'arte was for Molière and many others.

These limitations and restrictions within traditional theatre study had become so obvious and so troublesome by the later 20th century that the time had clearly arrived for a major reorientation of the field to respond to them. In short, what Kuhn called a 'paradigm shift' was required in the Western understanding of what theatre was. Performance studies provided the major mechanism for this shift, opening the concept of theatre to a more global perspective, to a more democratic one, and to one which moved the focus of theatre from the dramatic text to the entire event of which its presentation was one part, and in some cases not even an essential part.

One might characterize these major shifts as that performance encouraged in theatre as internationalization, democratization, and contextualization.

International performance

Despite its close ties to its particular culture, an important part of world theatre has always had an international element. Touring individuals and companies can be traced to classical times in both Europe and Asia. The travelling commedia companies created a performance web across Europe in the Renaissance and Baroque periods, and improved transportation allowed the great actors of the late 19th century and the great companies of the early 20th century to be seen by audiences around the globe. This process continued to extend all during that century as both communication and transportation improved. By the early 1960s many persons concerned with theatre would have agreed that the growing international attention of the the influential journal *TDR* was expressing the developing international awareness of the field. At that time, developing an international awareness for Anglo-Saxon, especially United States, students of theatre basically meant moving outside their own tradition to consider artists like Artaud and Grotowski, but later issues of *TDR* moved on beyond the traditional Eurocentric model to consider other areas of the world such as Latin America and Asia. In this, *TDR*, as it so often did during those years, both reflected and encouraged important new concerns in Western theatre studies in general. During the next two decades, as Schechner was developing his ideas on performance, these were profoundly influenced by his study of rituals and other performance activities in New Guinea and India. Doubtless the increasing globalization of culture during these years would have led to a greater awareness of theatre practices around the world even without the particular influence of *TDR* and the rise of performance studies, but it is also undeniable that the insights and strategies developed within performance studies both reinforced and profoundly influenced this tendency.

A focus upon performance was particularly important in countering a major obstacle in the development of a more global understanding and appreciation of theatre. This is a problem created by the success of colonialism. Wherever the great colonial empires spread, especially those of England, France, and Spain, which eventually covered much of the globe, European patterns of culture, including the theatre, were imposed or at least held up as superior models for local artists to imitate. Previous local forms of public entertainment or celebrations were generally ignored as backward or insignificant. Thus, for example, both European and Arabic histories of the theatre still generally report that theatre is unknown to the Arab world until introduced by the presentation of a Molière-style play in Beirut in 1847, dismissing centuries of public performances—storytelling, puppet theatre, comic sketches, and so on—that did not fit the standard 19th century European idea of theatre. Similar situations could be cited from around the world. Thus, thanks to colonialism, theatre scholars could, until very recently, consider themselves quite international by studying dramatic works from Africa, south and east Asia, the Middle East, and Latin America without ever leaving the comfortable and familiar models of the European tradition, faithfully imitated by colonial authors in all of these areas.

The rise of post-colonial theatre challenged these comfortable assumptions and performance studies provided a way for theatre scholars to move beyond them, and to approach types of cultural expression that did follow the standard European model of theatre, but offered an equally rich and complex experience to their society.

Many of the performance traditions outside the Western norms did not place the literary text at the centre of their experience.

8. Theyyam ritual, Kerala, India

Thus the reorientation that performance offered, no longer viewing theatre as the embodiment of a pre-existing piece of literature but rather as a cultural and social event, a particular experience, proved particularly liberating (Figure 8). Closely related to this, of course, was the dissolving of the traditional idea of European high culture and the centrality of the canon, both serious obstacles to understanding and evaluating performance events from other cultures and also to recognizing the importance of the many non-literary theatrical activities in the popular culture of the so-called Western nations themselves. Finally, performance studies contributed importantly to a new way of thinking about theatre, not as an isolated artistic object but as an experience embedded in cultural processes. A key book in articulating this shift was Gerald Hinkle's 1979 *Art as Event*, which argued that a true understanding of the performing arts had been hampered by the application to them of analytic strategies evolved in arts like literature or painting. The major difference, of course, is performance, the recognition of which forces an analytic shift from an object in perception to an episode in experience.

Although Hinkle was neither a theatre nor performance scholar, but a professor of philosophy, his insight is wholly in line with that articulated during this decade by Schechner in developing his concept of performance. One can see how close Schechner is to Hinkle in such statements as his distinction of drama, script, theatre, and performance in an essay of that name from 1973. Here he defined drama as the text originally created by the playwright, the script as the particular form created from that text for a particular production; the theatre as the movements and gestures of the performers enacting that script, and the performance (just as Hinkle saw it) as the entire event, including audience, performers, technicians—everyone present. This shift in analytical perspective from theatre as an object to theatre as an event, implied in the stress on performance, has been of enormous importance in subsequent theatre studies.

Thus the increasingly common affiliation of theatre with performance, especially in the disciplinary concerns, goes far beyond an interest in the rather narrow type of activity called 'performance art' which flourished in the late 20th century and has since distinctly diminished in importance. It also goes beyond the much more central association of these two terms in modern times which has insisted that the physical realization of the play on stage, that is, its performance, was essential to an understanding of theatre. What the concept of performance, as it has been developed since the 1960s, has added to these associations is a recognition that especially if theatre is to be considered as a particular kind of human activity found in many cultures, it needs to be considered in a very wide variety of manifestations, and in relation to other related cultural activities, such as rituals, festivals, civic demonstrations, dances, puppet shows, circuses, and storytelling. Performance has offered to the theatre a view of human activity that allows it to escape from the restricted model of a particular cultural activity of late 19th century Europe and its cultural satellites, and become open to something closer to a global consideration of the theatre, an increasingly important concern in an increasingly interconnected world.

Chapter 5
The makers of theatre

One of the most distinctive features of theatre and of its sister art opera is the wide variety of people involved in its creation. One normally thinks of an artwork as being brought into existence by a single artist—the poet, the painter, the architect, the musician— but even though the playwright usually (though not always) works alone, when his or her play is converted into theatre, an entire group of other contributors is required. In this section we will examine the role of those other contributors and what they bring or have brought to the theatre in different eras of history and different parts of the world.

The actor

The actor is clearly the central contributor to almost every form of theatre. If we return again to Eric Bentley's basic definition of theatre: 'A impersonates B while C looks on,' we might note that it is not only a definition of theatre but of the art of acting. As soon as one human being stands up before others and pretends to be something or someone else, both acting and theatre are created. In this most basic form, theatre need not even be a group creation; the single artist, the actor, presents his creation directly to a public, just as the painter or poet can do. Normally, of course, the actor is supported by a wide range of other artists, the designers who provide his dress and his physical surroundings, the playwright who supplies his words, the director who places him in a particular conceptual world, and so on. I will discuss each of these other contributors in turn, but clearly it is with the actor that one must begin.

There is evidence of acting going back to the earliest human civilization. A mysterious figure, usually called the 'Sorcerer', found on the wall of The Three Brothers Cave in France, is generally thought to portray a shaman or a performer dressed in the skin and antlers of a deer, in short, engaged in role playing. The figure dates from the Stone Age, around 13,000 BCE (Figure 9). Aristotle places the birth of theatre at that time when an individual performer, Thespis, stepped out of the Dionysiac chorus and took on the role of a specific character. In his honour, actors in the West are still often referred to as 'thespians'. Although the chorus remained an important part of the classical Greek theatre, the actor steadily increased in relative importance. In the 5th century BCE Aeschylus added a second actor, allowing a conversation which did not involve the chorus, and Sophocles added a third, but no more were added in the classical period. At first the playwrights themselves played the leading actor, but by the end of the century professional actors played all three roles.

Both male and female roles were played by men, but in general classical Greek theatre had little concern with realism. The actors all wore stylized costumes, large masks, and elevated shoes, which gave the impression that they were larger than life. The custom of performing in traditional costumes and masks carried over into the Roman theatre and was continued in the Roman pantomimes of the late classical theatre. So close was the association of the mask with this art form that still today a stylized representation of the masks of tragedy and comedy is a standard symbol for theatre.

The first major theatre form in Asia, the Sanskrit theatre, used no masks, but these were common in the later dance drama forms

9. Costumed performer on the walls of the Paleolithic Cave of the Three Brothers, France

developed from this tradition. Both male and female actors performed, drawn from the religious community, priests and temple attendants. By the 11th century women's performances took place only within the temples, while men could also perform outside. In general, from the medieval period onward, theatre in Europe gradually became more realistic, and such formal elements as masks and dance tended to disappear (except in certain court spectacles and interludes, and in the tradition of the partially masked commedia dell'arte). In most of the rest of the world, however, at least until the colonial period, theatrical performance, often closely tied to ritual, remained on the whole much more closely connected to such formal elements, as did the art of acting itself. The tradition of the masked performer was maintained in the Noh drama and in such forms as the Korean *Talchum*, which literally means 'mask dance'; and in other forms, such as Kabuki or the southern Indian Kathikali, elaborate mask-like makeup gave a similar impression, reinforced by richly decorative traditional costuming. West Africa, and especially Nigeria, has an important tradition of masked dance drama, as does Latin America, and especially Mexico and Guatemala.

Although there are a few instances of women appearing on stage during the European Middle Ages, they did not appear regularly until the mid 16th century in Spain and Italy, around 1600 in France and with the Restoration in England in 1660. Before that time, most notably in the Shakespearian theatre, women's roles were played by boys and young men. This practice has been occasionally revived in modern times for Elizabethan work, as in the restored Globe Theatre in London today. The dominance of realism in the West however, has since the 17th century reinforced male and female casting. There have been notable exceptions, however, such as the breeches roles, putting women in men's dress, which have been popular, especially in England, since women first appeared on British stages, and various forms of 'drag' roles, with men appearing as women. Both of these, of course, have been an important part of theatrical explorations of gender in recent times.

In many periods and cultures actors have performed alone, but more normally they have appeared as part of a group or company, and until recent times most such groups remained fairly stable over long periods. In some cases, most notably in the travelling commedia dell'arte companies of the Renaissance, they consisted of members of a single family or closely related families. This pattern remained standard until the late 19th century, when leading actors like Sarah Bernhardt found it more to their economic advantage to temporarily join with whatever group could offer the best opportunities. Today, especially in the United States, companies of actors who remain together for extended periods are a quite minor part of the theatre scene, and in most cases, actors are assembled for a single production and then disperse.

This has disrupted the traditional master–apprentice system of actor training that is still found in most parts of the world and makes both the education and the employment of actors in the United States a very unstable system. Another effect of the long-established company was to encourage actors to repeat certain types of roles or relationships in a variety of plays, so that an actor would present a certain 'type' or 'line of business' such as playing innocent maidens or benevolent old men. Until well into the 19th century, many playwrights created plays built around these types and their established relationships.

With the coming of Romanticism, however, and the championship of individual artistic insight, the old system of following expectations of type began to disappear. The 'Romantic' actor was not only noted for his emotionality but for his unpredictability and for his willingness to interpret traditional roles, like those of Shakespeare, in highly unconventional ways. Whereas the 18th century actor was praised, like the actors of the classical Japanese stage, for the intensity and the emotional power which he brought to a traditional style of performance, the Romantic actor sought to achieve these effects through his originality.

Not uncoincidentally, the late 18th century European theorists began to consider for the first time the role of the emotions in acting, a consideration that did not arise so long as acting was considered primarily the effective repetition of well-established gestures, tones, and attitudes. Denis Diderot most famously articulated this position with his famous 'paradox' that the best actor was the one who actually felt little, but possessed the technical skill to exactly imitate emotion. The Romantic actor instead sought to build his acting upon emotions actually felt and these opposing positions, acting from the 'head' or from the 'heart', have echoed through Western acting theory and training ever since. The theorist most associated with the utilization of emotion was doubtless Constantin Stanislavsky, director of the Moscow Art Theatre at the end of the 19th century. His concept of the actor 'living the role' was the primary source of American 'method' acting, which became the major approach for actors interpreting the realistic dramas that dominated the 20th century in the West.

Although in modern times popular actors have achieved enormous visibility and social status, for most of history and in many parts of the world their social position was a precarious one. When protected by monarchs and other rulers they were at best a kind of court functionary, serving at the behest of their royal masters, but much more frequently they existed on the margins of society. The Kabuki theatre began as essentially a display of prostitutes, and actresses have often, justly or not, been suspected of this trade. The Western Church almost from the beginning has been suspicious of the craft of acting, and has often forbidden actors the sacraments or participation in religious activities. Only during the 19th century did the acting profession gain general social respectability in Europe, and even today the actor or actress, whatever their fame and prominence, still often carries a faintly bohemian aura for much of the public.

It is the adventures and interactions of these engaging, mysterious, mercurial, erotic creatures, the actors, in some ways deeply reflecting ourselves and in others strangely alien, which have always formed the basis of the theatre.

The puppet

It may seem odd to a Western reader to accord a special section to the puppet, but should we consider only the performance of living actors, we would have to omit a very significant part of the world's theatre. There is no part of the world in which a significant tradition of puppet theatre does not exist, and in Asia it rivals the theatre of the living actor in importance. Toy animals and human figures with parts moved by string, which may or may not have been used to tell stories, have been found in Egypt and the Indus Valley dating back to before 2000 BCE. The first record of inanimate figures utilized to tell stories, however, comes from Greece in the 5th century BCE, the same period that saw the full flowering of the live theatre there. The dolls were usually terracotta figures, manipulated by strings. Three centuries later Tamil puppet performances are recorded in southern India. Most of the world's puppets are manipulated by a single operator, most often from above, using strings, or from below, using rods or other supports. The major exception is the Japanese Bunraku, whose large puppets are each manipulated by three visible but black-clad puppeteers, one controlling the head and right arm, another the left arm, and a third the feet and legs.

Puppets controlled from above by strings began to be called marionettes around 1600 in Italy, although their use in both Italy and France has been recorded for three centuries before that. As early as the 13th century, wooden puppets presented the *Opera dei Pupi*, based on troubadour poems, in Sicily, a tradition which still exists today. The early commedia dell'arte is thought by many to have been strongly influenced by this tradition and it in turn inspired the British figure of Punch, who is first recorded in 1662 and has become a prominent part of British culture. Although many other forms of puppetry have been and are performed in Europe, the marionette has been the dominant one. Chaucer, in the late 14th century, notes the use of puppets in England, and they were a common entertainment in aristocratic homes and fairs by Elizabethan times, most notably serving as the basis of a key scene in Ben Jonson's 1614 *Bartholomew Fair*.

Marionettes have always been an important part of the European theatre, although rarely given much attention by traditional theatre historians. During the 18th century, Punch and Judy shows were among the most popular theatrical entertainments in England, and were successfully exported to the continent and to America. In central Europe, marionette operas were an extremely popular form and that tradition is still honoured today in the Salzburg Marionette Theatre, founded in 1913.

The commedia character Pulcinella, who inspired Punch in England, was also the inspiration for the French character Polichinelle, who first appeared in 1804 and was soon overshadowed by his fellow marionette Guignol, whose popularity in France soon rivalled that of Punch in England. Toward the end of the 19th century, symbolist theorists and dramatists championed the marionette as an abstract figure that could tap into the deeper currents of the universe than could the more individualist human actor, and moreover, would be completely under the control of the director, a theatrical figure whose total control over the production was an important part of symbolist theory. The theatrical superiority of the marionette over the actor, suggested as early as 1810 in a famous essay by the German Romantic Heinrich von Kleist, was promulgated most famously by Edward Gordon Craig in his 1908 'The Actor and the Über-Marionette'. During the 20th century European-style marionette theatre remained an important element of theatre on that continent and spread as far as Australia.

In east Asia and the Middle East, the dominant form of puppet theatre has not been the marionette, but the shadow puppet, which utilizes two-dimensional puppets manipulated from below and backlit against a translucent screen to form images. Shadow puppetry is said to have originated in China under the emperor

Wu of the Han dynasty in the 1st century BCE. It remained a major art form during succeeding dynasties and of the Mongols, who conquered China in the 13th century. The Mongols in turn carried the form with them into other parts of their expanding empire, most importantly into central Asia and the Middle East.

Until modern times there was a thriving shadow puppet theatre tradition in India, probably originally imported from China, but the major home of shadow puppetry today is south-east Asia, which imported this art from India or China. Malaysia, Cambodia, and Thailand all have active shadow theatre, but the best known is the *wayang kulit* of Indonesia, whose intricately cut and decorated figures are almost as familiar a symbol of south-east Asian theatre as the Greek masks are of Western theatre.

The other major area for the development of shadow puppetry has been the Middle East. Scholars agree that the shadow theatre was brought to Turkey from Egypt in the 16th century and from there spread over the Ottoman Empire, giving rise to a number of puppet traditions still active today, headed by the Turkish karagoz, but how the form developed in Egypt is much disputed. Some, recalling the puppets of ancient Egypt, argue that it developed there without Asian influence, while others, noting that Arab merchants were active in Indonesia as early as the 5th century, have suggested a borrowing from that part of the world. In any case, the form was well established in Egypt by the 10th century, and remained the dominant theatre form there for centuries. At the end of the 13th century, the Egyptian dramatist Ibn Daniyal created for this theatre some of the most sophisticated medieval dramas produced anywhere in the world.

Although these two basic types of puppets have been the most common, many other varieties are found in the dozens of countries around the world with a strong puppet tradition, from the hand and arm puppets that as Muppets have made a major impact on American film, stage, and television, to the exotic water puppets of

Thailand, seeming to move on the water but controlled by rods beneath its surface. Together the puppets and their manipulators continue to be among the leading makers of world theatre.

The designer

The first actors presumably performed in the open air, then in front of such neutral backgrounds as hanging cloths, and then before fairly neutral architectural backgrounds, as we see in the Sanskrit stage or the classical theatres of Greece and Rome. According to Aristotle, the decoration of this neutral background began as early as Sophocles, who, Aristotle asserts, 'invented scene painting'. The designer did not emerge as a significant theatre artist in the West until the Renaissance, however, when the courts first of Italy, then of France and elsewhere, encouraged lavish scenic spectacles in the theatre and outside, as a display of their wealth and power. Major artists such as Leonardo da Vinci designed for these theatres, and frequently the designer far surpassed the actor in his contribution to the theatre event.

The same is true of the lavish English court entertainments called masques, which, under continental influence flourished at the English court during the Renaissance. The first great English stage designer, Inigo Jones, famously quarrelled with playwright Ben Jonson over whose art was more central in such works, with the performers largely forgotten. This question did not arise for the works of Shakespeare, from the same period, since these were created for the public theatre, whose essentially neutral background needed no contribution from a scenic artist.

This continued to be the case with the neoclassical spoken theatre in general. During the 17th and 18th centuries, Europe saw a great flourishing of scenic design, but this was largely created for operas, court spectacles, or simply for lavish engravings. These designs epitomized Baroque splendor—formidable and intricate compositions, almost entirely architectural, and replacing the single vanishing point perspective of Renaissance designers with striking multiple perspectives. The Bibiena family of Italy and the Galli family with which they united, were the favourite designers for the Hapsburg courts and the dominant figures in European design for these two centuries.

The Japanese Noh drama, with its traditional and basically unchanging stage, does not really require a scenic designer, but the Kabuki and Bunraku during the 18th century turned more and more to visual spectacle and elaborate machinery, which then became an important part of the theatre experience. The major names associated with this spectacle were not, however, designers, but the playwrights themselves—Edo dramatist Nakamura Denshichi or Kanai Shozo.

Romanticism brought a completely different style to the European theatre, and unlike Baroque design had a profound influence on spoken drama as well as the opera. The first important representative of this new approach was Philip James de Loutherbourg, who was not trained in architectural design, like the Bibienas, but as a landscape painter. Working in London with the leading actor David Garrick, he introduced not only more natural settings, but a new interest in mood and atmosphere. He was the first to employ the recently discovered Argand lamp to help achieve these effects and so may be considered the first lighting designer as well.

Scenic designers achieved new prominence in the theatre and the opera of the early 19th century, offering visual spectacle in the new Romantic style, like the famous erupting volcanos of Alessandro Sanquirico at Milan's La Scala or the monumental staircases or ghostly cloisters created in Paris by Pierre Ciceri. The stage machinist, such as Henri Duponchel, who worked with Ciceri, emerged at this time as another important theatrical collaborator, and as the century progressed would sometimes be listed among the leading artists for a production. The detailed historicism of Charles Kean's Shakespearian productions in the 1830s continued to influence the monumental settings of the rest of the century, culminating in the productions of Henry Irving and Beerbohm Tree. All these leading directors worked with a number of designers, often creating different settings for the same production.

Although costume had been a part of the actor's presentation since the art began, it was not until the 19th century that the costume designer was generally recognized as an important contributor to the overall production. A leader in establishing this position was James Planché, who convinced Charles Kean of the importance of historical costuming, beginning with his 1846 *King John*.

A major reaction against such elaborately decorative realism took place at the opening of the 20th century, calling for a more simplified and evocative style called the 'new stagecraft'. Its leaders were Adolphe Appia of Switzerland and Edward Gordon Craig from England, and their writings and designs gave the scene designer a new prominence in the 20th century. Such designers as Robert Edmond Jones or Jo Mielziner in the United States, Caspar Neher or Wilfried Minks in Germany, Motley or John Napier in England, or Alexandra Exter in Russia have gained renown equal to the actors and directors with whom they worked.

In the late 20th century artists like Robert Wilson from the United States, Josef Svoboda of Czechoslovakia, Jerzy Grotowski of Poland, and Andreas Kriegenberg of Germany have become equally well known as designers and directors.

Ever since the founders of the new stagecraft, headed by Appia, insisted upon the centrality of light in the theatre, the lighting designer has been recognized as another important contributor to the creation of the modern theatre. Although sound has been a part of theatrical performance since the art began, the first person to be designated a sound designer was Dan Dugan, at the

American Conservatory Theatre in San Francisco in 1968. Today both musical and spoken plays regularly include sound designers among their central artists, to supervise the design, installation, and calibration of the aural effects. As theatre has more and more utilized other media, still other contributors to it are often added as well—especially such visual contributors as projectionists, video and film artists, puppeteers, and creators of digital effects. Today theatre designers may make up a very large part of the creative team.

The director

Since theatre normally requires the combined work of a number of artists, it also usually requires someone to coordinate this work, a director, unless its performance traditions are so well established, as in the classical Japanese Noh and Kabuki, that no such guiding hand is necessary. In the classical Greek theatre, this function was served by the dramatist, and that practice has been often followed in long-established theatres where dramatists, actors, and theatre organizations have an ongoing relationship, as for example in the French theatre of the 19th century. Sometimes, most notably in the cases of Aeschylus and Molière, the playwright served not only as director, but as leading actor. In the Sanskrit theatre and in many related Indian forms there is a similar figure, the *sutradhara*, a name which, in obvious reference to the marionette theatre, literally means 'the holder of strings'. He orchestrates the prayers and opening rituals, and appears as a performer in the prologue and framing scenes, but he also serves as the overall organizer and manager of the production.

It has usually been the custom in travelling companies, from the commedia dell'arte onward into the 19th century, that the leading actor, the capocomico, served also as director. A similar role was that of the actor-manager, which appeared in the late 16th century and still may be occasionally found today, where a star actor assembles his own company and presents works in his own theatre. Most of the leading actors of 19th century Europe, such as Henry Irving and Sarah Bernhardt, worked under this arrangement.

In the early 20th century, the actor-manager was generally replaced in the Western theatre by the modern director, who supervises all aspects of production, from time to time also serves as designer, but normally serves neither as an actor or designer. The model for this position was developed in 19th century Germany by such artists as Goethe and George II, Duke of Saxe-Meiningen, and brought to its fullest manifestation at the beginning of the next century by artists like Max Reinhardt in Germany, David Belasco in the United States, and by the great generation of Russian Revolutionary directors headed by Constantin Stanislavski and Vsevolod Meyerhold (Figure 10).

At this same time, theorists like the British designer Edward Gordon Craig advanced the concept of the director as the master artist of the theatre, providing it with a unity and totality of vision

10. **David Belasco with his stage designers and technicians, 1912**

such as that described by Richard Wagner as a 'total work of art' (*Gesamtkunstwerk*). This concept spread throughout the Western theatre during the 20th century, and spread from there to Western-oriented theatres around the world, with the result that the 20th century has often been called the 'age of the director'. Whereas in earlier centuries the best-known theatre artists had been playwrights, actors, or occasionally designers, the best-known theatre artists of the late 20th century were largely directors: France's Ariane Mnouchkine, Patrice Chereau, and Peter Brook (who began his career in England), Germany's Peter Stein, Peter Zadek, and Frank Castorf, Italy's Giorgio Strehler, Spain's Nuria Espert and Calixto Bieito, Peter Sellars and Robert Wilson from the United States, Brazil's Augusto Boal, Israel's Yuri Lyobimov, Japan's Tadashi Suzuki, Poland's Jerzy Grotowski. With the ease of international travel, many of these became as well known around the globe as they were in their native country.

The modern director often operates not simply as the coordinator of the work of other artists, but as a creative artist in his or her own right, often producing interpretations of older works radically at odds with tradition. This tendency has been called *Regietheater* by the Germans and is usually traced back to the post-World War II productions by Wieland Wagner of the works of his grandfather, Richard Wagner, in highly untraditional minimalist and abstract designs, based on the suggestions of the visionary designer Adolph Appia.

Traditionalists have often attacked the liberties taken by *Regietheater* directors, but such work still dominates the theatres of continental Europe, especially of the German-speaking countries, while directors in England and the United States have, on the whole, followed the more conventional stage approaches of the last century. The notable exceptions, like JoAnne Akalaitis or Robert Wilson, pursue their work almost entirely in minor theatres or abroad. As a result English or United States productions are generally publicized and spoken of in terms of their actors, unlike the situation in Germany, where the director's name is normally dominant.

The audience

It may seem surprising to find the audience included among the 'makers of theatre', since the normal idea of theatre is that it is 'made' by a group of 'artists' *for* an audience. Recall the minimal definition of theatre by Eric Bentley cited near the beginning of this book: 'A impersonates B while C looks on.' While this minimal formula indeed covers a very wide range of world theatre, its presupposition of a totally passive C is by no means universal. The Western theatre has largely assumed that the theatre was made on the stage and presented as a finished product to an audience, who simply absorbed what was presented to them. This assumption was reinforced with the rise of the modern realistic theatre, which emphasized the passivity of the audience by darkening the auditorium and generally discouraging any active audience response to the performance except for laughter and occasional applause.

Many non-Western traditions allow for and indeed expect more active audience participation. The contemporary South African performer Chantal Snyman has called a high degree of audience participation one of the major characteristics of African theatre in general, and the work of artists like Hope Azeda of Rwanda, Mumpuh Kwachuh of Cameroon, Frederick Philander of Namibia, and Cheela Chilala of Zambia provide clear support for this assertion. Within the Arab world, the traditional *halqa* performances, named for the circle the audience forms around the actors, are similarly strongly involved with audience participation, a fact recognized in the contemporary dramas of playwrights from Tayeb Saddiki in Morocco to Sa'dallah Wannous in Syria, who have created modern plays utilizing traditional *halqa* audience participation. In Brazil, the highly influential theatre artist and theorist Augusto Boal developed a variety of strategies to involve audiences directly, always with a sociopolitical goal. His best-known such approach was the Forum Theatre, developed in the 1970s and highly influential around the world. Here the spectators were converted into what Boal called 'spec-actors' who were encouraged to take over the process of creating the text being performed. Similar strategies have become common in politically engaged theatre companies in many countries today.

A major theoretical shift in the late 20th century also distinctly changed the traditional Western view of theatre audiences. This was reception theory, developed from the writings of German theorists Wolfgang Iser and Hans-Robert Jauss in the 1960s. Within theatre, this approach insisted that audiences, far from being passive recipients, were actively involved in the creation of meaning, not at all necessarily what the artists themselves intended. The theatre event came to be seen as co-created by the performers and the audience, and the audience in fact joined actors and other artists as collaborative 'makers' of the experience. This approach received powerful support in 2008 from a widely quoted article by French theorist Jacques Rancière entitled 'The Emancipated Spectator', which stressed the capacity of audience members to create their own meanings from material presented to them.

Generally speaking, when reception theory has spoken of audiences as co-creators, which it often has, it has focused upon the process of reception and the fact that an audience singly or collectively could interpret a work of art quite differently from what the artists intended. This process is fairly clear when one is speaking of a work of literature or a painting, but a different dynamic is possible in theatre, where the audience is actively present during the creative process and thus capable of actually taking a hand in it.

The Forum Theatre of Augusto Boal points toward a more radical way in which audiences can join in the process of making theatre, and that is to provide them with actual agency in determining the theatre event itself. In various forms, this dynamic has been seen in a significant amount of experimental theatre in the late 20th and early 21st centuries, especially in Europe and the United States. Some, strongly political in orientation, have closely followed the Boal model, presenting audiences with a piece of pre-written script and then allowing them to decide how the characters and situation will develop. Two important examples are the West Bengal company Jana Sanskriti, formed in 1985, which has spread Forum Theatre across India. The Cardboard Company, created in London in 1991, has spread these techniques internationally, as has Boal himself, establishing this form of audience theatre creation as far as Melbourne, Australia. Forum procedures have also been adopted by non-political commercial theatres, as may be seen in the Broadway musical by Rupert Holmes, *The Mystery of Edwin Drood*, which in 1985 allowed audiences to create their own endings, different every night, for this adaptation of an unfinished novel by Charles Dickens.

A rather different type of audience interaction grows out of a practice which goes back to experimental productions of the early 20th century in Russia, which mixed audiences among the actors, although without giving them the power to actually shape the performance. The Polish director Jerzy Grotowski converted audience members into guests at Faust's table in his production of that play, and into patients in a psychiatric hospital which was the setting of his production *Kordian*. Inspired by Grotowski's work, Richard Schechner in his 1969 *Dionysius in 69* sought to create theatre which he called 'not an aesthetic but a social event', in which actors and spectators were encouraged to mix and interact.

In 2000, as the new century began, a new company in London, Punchdrunk, began offering an even more open opportunity for audience structuring of the theatre experience, in what it called 'immersive theatre'. The enormous success of Punchdrunk's production of *Sleep No More*, primarily inspired by Shakespeare's

Macbeth, especially after it was restaged in New York in 2009, caused a major vogue of immersive productions in London and New York, and subsequently in many other world theatre centres. Immersive theatre, as I noted in my opening chapter, grew out of the international interest in site-specific theatre in the late 20th century, although it also has close ties to installation art and immersive video games. Although early site-specific performances simply gathered audiences in locations outside conventional theatre spaces, they generally expected audiences to remain seated and passive, as they were in traditional theatre situations. During the 1980s a number of theatres, especially in England, began to present plays in multiple locations, among which the audience had to circulate. The leader in such work, generally called promenade theatre or walkabouts, was and remains the Duke's Theatre in Lancaster, which staged its first walkabout in 1987, *A Midsummer Night's Dream*.

Immersive theatre extends the idea of the walkabout, giving the audience much more latitude in creating their own experience. Instead of being guided to a specific series of prearranged scenes, they are set free to wander as they please in a large environment, like an abandoned factory or warehouse, containing many individualized spaces, often elaborately decorated, which may or may not contain actual performers. Most immersive productions contain a central action, although how much of this an individual audience member may see occurs partly by chance and partly by the choice of that member. In *Sleep No More* audiences are discouraged from interacting with the performers or indeed with each other, while in *Speakeasy Dollhouse*, which opened in New York in 2011, such interaction is encouraged and when a murder takes place in the world of the play, the audience members are questioned by the police as witnesses.

Although still centred in England and the United States, immersive theatre, thanks to the internationalization of experimental performance, is spreading around the globe. Argentina's first such company, Usted Está Aqu66, was founded in Buenos Aires in 2012, and the form has proven particularly popular in Australia. Indeed, an organization, Interactive Theatre Australia, was formed in Brisbane in 1997 and in 2010 became Interactive Theatre International, marking the global interest in such work. Perhaps the most outstanding interactive or immersive theatre group in the world today is Signa, founded in Copenhagen, Denmark in 2001. Their best-known production, *The Ruby-Town Oracle*, was performed in Cologne and Berlin in 2007. Here an entire gypsy village was created in a presumed neutral zone where visitors needed passports to enter. Although the town had a constructed history, as did the performing inhabitants, there was no text. During the eight days of non-stop performance, audience members could come and go at will, and interact with the 'inhabitants' in any way they chose, chatting, gossiping, flirting, sleeping, eating, and drinking. The experience was similar to being a tourist in a small village in an unfamiliar country and spectators could either perform themselves or if they wished take on a different persona entirely. The action was whatever they could negotiate with either the inhabitants or other visitors.

Despite the growing popularity of these different types of interactive theatre, most of the world's theatre experience remains close to the core active–passive–mimetic structure laid out by Bentley. Nevertheless, a growing fascination with participation and intervention, surely fuelled by the popularity of interactive video, has already seriously changed the dynamics of the theatre around the world and will doubtless remain an important new part of the theatrical experience in the years to come. In a more literal sense than ever before, then, the audience will be regarded as one of the central makers of theatre.

Further reading

The following list provides a sampling of the leading texts on various aspects of theatre in English and also serves as an acknowledgement of some of the main sources used in the present book.

Appia, Adolphe, *Essays, Scenarios, and Designs*, trans. Walter R. Volbach, Research Press, Ann Arbor, MI, 1989.

Arnott, Peter, *The Ancient Greek and Roman Theatre*, Random House, New York, 1971.

Arnott, Peter, *An Introduction to the French Theatre*, Rowan and Littlefield, Totowa, NJ, 1977.

Artaud, Antonin, *The Theatre and Its Double*, trans. M. C. Richard, Grove, New York, 1958.

Aston, Elaine and George Savona, *Theatre as Sign-System: A Semiotics of Text and Performance*, Routledge, London, 1991.

Austin, J. L., *How to Do Things with Words*, Harvard University Press, Cambridge, MA, 1975.

Balme, Christopher, *Decolonizing the Stage*, Oxford University Press, Oxford, 1999.

Banham, Martin, ed., *A History of Theatre in Africa*, Cambridge University Press, New York, 2004.

Barish, Jonas, *The Antitheatrical Prejudice*, University of California Press, Berkeley, 1985.

Bentley, Eric, *The Life of the Drama*, Atheneum, New York, 1964.

Bieber, Margarete, *The History of Greek and Roman Theatre*, 2nd edn, Princeton University Press, Princeton, NJ, 1961.

Blumenthal, Eileen, *Puppetry and Puppets*, Thames & Hudson, London, 2005.

Boal, Augusto, *Theatre of the Oppressed*, trans. Charles A. McBride, Urizen books, 1979.

Bowers, Faubion, *Theatre in the East: A Survey of Asian Dance and Drama*, Grove, New York, 1969.

Brandon, James, *On Thrones of Gold: Three Javanese Shadow Plays*, Harvard University Press, Cambridge, MA, 1970.

Brandon, James, ed., *The Cambridge Guide to Asian Theatre*, Cambridge University Press, New York, 1993.

Brockett, Oscar, and Robert Findlay, *Century of Innovation: A History of European and American Theatre and Drama since the Late Nineteenth Century*, 2nd edn, Allyn and Bacon, Boston, MA, 1991.

Brockett, Oscar, with Franklin J. Hildy, *History of the Theatre*, 9th edn, Allyn and Bacon, Boston, MA, 2003.

Brockett, Oscar, Margaret A. Mitchell, and Linda Hardenberger, *Making the Scene: A History of Stage Design and Technology in Europe and the United States*, University of Texas Press, Austin, 2010.

Brook, Peter, *The Empty Space: A Book about the Theatre*, Touchstone, New York, 1968.

Bulman, Gail A., *Staging Words, Playing Worlds: Intertextuality and Nation in Contemporary Latin American Theatre*, Bucknell University Press, Lewistown, PA, 2007.

Burke, Kenneth, *A Grammar of Motives*, Prentice-Hall, New York, 1945.

Burke, Kenneth, *A Rhetoric of Motives*, G. Braziller, New York, 1955.

Burns, Elizabeth, *Theatricality: A Study of Convention in the Theatre and in Social Life*, Longman, London, 1972.

Butler, James, *The Theatre and Drama of Greece and Rome*, Chandler, San Francisco, 1972.

Carlson, Marvin, *Places of Performance: The Semiotics of Theatre Architecture*, Cornell University Press, Ithaca, NY, 1989.

Carlson, Marvin, *Theories of the Theatre: A Historical and Critical Survey from the Greeks to the Present*, expanded edn, Cornell University Press, Ithaca, NY, 1993.

Carlson, Marvin, *Performance, A Critical Introduction*, Routledge, London, 1998.

Chambers, E. K., *The Medieval Stage*, 2 vols, Clarendon, Oxford, 1903.

Chambers, E. K., *The Elizabethan Stage*, 4 vols, Clarendon, Oxford, 1965.

Chelkowski, Peter J., ed., *Eternal Performance: Ta'ziyeh and other Shiite rituals*, Seagull Books, London, 2010.

Cole, Toby and Helen K. Chinoy, eds, *Actors on Acting*, rev. edn, Crown, New York, 1980.

Cole, Toby and Helen K. Chinoy, *Directors on Directing*, Macmillan, New York, 1985.

Craig, Edward Gordon, *On the Art of the Theatre*, Brown's Bookstore, Chicago, 1911.

Dolan, Jill, *The Feminist Spectator as Critic*, University of Michigan Press, Ann Arbor, MI, 1991.

Dolby, William, *A History of the Chinese Drama*, Harper and Row, New York, 1976.

Ducharte, Pierre, *The Italian Comedy*, trans. R. T. Weaver, Dover, New York, 1966.

Evreinoff, Nikolas, *The Theatre in Life*, trans. Alexander Nazaroff, Brentano's, New York, 1927.

Fischer-Lichte, Erika, *The Transformative Power of Performance*, trans. Saslya Iris Jain, Routledge, New York, 2008.

Gargi, Balwant, *Theatre in India*, Theatre Arts, New York, 1962.

Gilbert, Helen and Joanne Tompkins, *Post-Colonial Drama: Theory, Practice, Politics*, Routledge, London, 1996.

Goffman, Erving, *The Presentation of Self in Everyday Life*, Doubleday, Garden City, NY, 1959.

Grotowski, Jerzy, *Towards a Poor Theatre*, Simon & Schuster, London, 1969.

Hardison, O. B., *Christian Rite and Christian Drama in the Middle Ages*, Johns Hopkins Press, Baltimore, 1965.

Hinkle, Gerard, *Art as Event*, University Press of American, Lanham, MA, 1979.

Hunninger, Ben, *The Origin of the Theater*, Hill and Wang, New York, 1961.

Innis, Christopher, *Avant-Garde TheatreTheatre, 1892–1992*, Routledge, New York, 1993.

Jackson, Shannon, *Professing Performance: Theatre in the Academy from Philology to Performativity*, Cambridge University Press, 2004.

Johnson, Harvey Leroy, *Introduction to the Jesuit Theatre*, ed. Louis I. Oldani, Institute of Jesuit Sources, St Louis, 1983.

Jurkowski, Henryk, *A History of English Puppetry*, Edwin Mellen Press, Lewiston, NY, 1996.

Kaprow, Allen, *Assemblages, Environments, and Happenings*, Harry N. Abrams, New York, 1966.

Kaye, Nick, *Site-Specific Art: Place and Documentation*, Routledge, London, 2000.

Kershaw, Baz, *The Radical in Performance: Between Brecht and Baudrillard*, Routledge, London, 1999.

Laver, James, *Drama: Its Costume and Décor*, Studio Publications, London, 1951.

Lehmann, Hans-Thies, *Postdramatic Theatre*, trans. Karen Jürs-Munby, Routledge, New York, 2006.

Leiris, Michel, *La Possession et ses aspect théâtraux chez les Ethiopiens de Gondar*, Plon, Paris, 1958.

Londré, Felicia Hardison and Daniel J. Watermeier, *The History of the North American Theater*, Continuum International Publishing, New York, 2000.

Mason, Bim, *Street Theatre and Other Outdoor Performance*, Routledge, London, 1992.

Ortolani, Benito, *The Japanese Theatre: From Shamanistic Ritual to Contemporary Pluralism*, rev. edn, Princeton University Press, Princeton, 1995.

Rancière, Jacques, *The Emancipated Spectator*, trans. Gregory Elliott, Verso, London, 2009.

Richmond, Farley, et al., *Indian Theatre: Traditions of Performance*, University of Hawaii Press, Honolulu, 1990.

Ridgeway, William, *The Drama and Dramatic Dances of Non-European Races*, Cambridge University Press, Cambridge, 1915.

Roach, Joseph, *Cities of the Dead*, Columbia University Press, New York, 1996.

Roose-Evans, James, *Experimental Thatre from Stanislavsky to Peter Brook*, Routledge, New York, 1996.

Rubin, Don, ed., *World Encyclopedia of Contemporary Theatre*, 5 vols, Routledge, New York, 1995–1999.

Schechner, Richard, *Environmental Theatre*, Hawthorne Books, New York, 1973.

Schechner, Richard, *Essays on Performance Theory 1970–1976*, Drama Book Specialists, New York, 1977.

Schechner, Richard, *Between Theatre and Anthropology*, University of Pennsylvania Press, Philadelphia, 1985.

Shergold, N. D., *A History of the Spanish Stage from Medieval Times until the End of the 17th Century*, Clarendon, Oxford, 1967.

Taylor, Diana, *The Archive and the Repertoire*, Duke University Press, Durham, NC, 2003.

Turner, Victor, *From Ritual to Theatre*, Performing Arts Journal Publications, New York, 1982.

Theatre

Tydeman, William, *English Medieval Theatre, 1400–1500*, Routledge and Kegan Paul, London, 1986.

Tydeman, William, Michael J. Anderson, and Nick Davis, eds, *The Medieval European Stage, 500–1550*, Cambridge University Press, Cambridge, 2001.

Vince, Ronald W., *Ancient and Medieval Theater: A Historiographical Handbook*, Greenwood, Westport, CT, 1984.

Vince, Ronald W., *Neoclassical Theater: A Historiographical Handbook*, Greenwood, Westport, CT, 1984.

Vince, Ronald W., *Renaissance Theater: A Historiographical Handbook*, Greenwood, Westport, CT, 1984.

Wiles, David, *Greek Theatre Performance*, Cambridge University Press, Cambridge, 2000.

Wilmeth, Don B. and Tice L. Miller, eds, *Cambridge Guide to American Theatre*, 2nd edn, Cambridge University Press, New York, 1996.

Winet, Evan, ed., *Indonesian Postcolonial Theatre*, Palgrave Macmillan, London, 2010.

Index

Index

Expand your collection of
VERY SHORT INTRODUCTIONS

SOCIAL MEDIA
Very Short Introduction

Join our community
www.oup.com/vsi

- Join us online at the official Very Short Introductions **Facebook** page.
- Access the thoughts and musings of our authors with our online **blog**.
- Sign up for our monthly **e-newsletter** to receive information on all new titles publishing that month.
- Browse the full range of Very Short Introductions online.
- Read **extracts** from the Introductions for free.
- Visit our library of **Reading Guides**. These guides, written by our expert authors will help you to question again, why you think what you think.
- If you are a teacher or lecturer you can order inspection copies quickly and simply via our website.

ONLINE CATALOGUE
A Very Short Introduction

Our online catalogue is designed to make it easy to find your ideal Very Short Introduction. View the entire collection by subject area, watch author videos, read sample chapters, and download reading guides.